This is no mere "winning-through" story. It is about how theology changes lives. It brings big doctrines into home and marriage and the choices we make every day. Very relevant and very good thinking.

Ann Benton

Writer and family conference speaker, Guildford, England

Lara Williams' testimony of God's faithfulness in the midst of the darkness of her broken marriage challenges and encourages us to take God at His Word. Full of rich Scriptural meditation in the midst of emotional devastation, Williams shows the path of having our thoughts and our lives transformed by the power of His Spirit and the light of His Word.

Diana Severance

Historian with broad experience in teaching in universities and seminaries, Spring, Texas

This is an amazing book! I'm all about helping marriages thrive, and through the unexpected and shattering experience of her husband's betrayal, Lara Williams triumphantly runs to God's Word instead of the divorce court and in the process discovers something we all desperately need. Letting go of our "rights," disappointments, and expectations of others liberates us to forgiveness, restoration, and trust. Her book will help transform your relationship with God which always leads to transformation with others.

Shaunti Feldhahn

Author of *For Women Only,* Norcross, Georgia

I've read lots of books on marriage but none of them have captured the beauty, lyrical quality, and biblical truth found here. Lara opens the shutters of her soul and lets us see the raw emotions and devastating hurt of betrayal fleshed out in gut level honesty. If you want a lasting love relationship that will go the distance, I highly recommend *To Walk or Stay*. This book is not data or theory. Lara writes out of the backyard of her own life and bares her soul.

Fred Lowery, PhD.

Pastor and Author of *Covenant Ma* ⬛⬛⬛⬛⬛, Louisiana

D1014356

What a story! This book is a terrific read on many levels. It is "real" and I am sure that most will relate to what this couple has gone through. To see how Lara dealt with the struggles in her marriage by choosing to turn towards God rather then give into her anger is truly inspiring. It will remind you of our most amazing God, who never fails to strengthen us in our time of need when we are blessed to turn to Him. A must read for all women.

Camille Franzese
Author of *This Thing of Ours,* Newport, California

"The miracle of a restored marriage is one miracle that God wants us to take an active part in celebrating. Lara's book definitely reveals this miracle. We *know* you will be encouraged as you read her story."

Dale and Jena Forehand
Founders of Stained Glass Ministries, Conference Leaders and author's of *Let's Get Real, Authentic Woman, and Living Deeper*, Birmingham, Alabama

Wow! How can you put words to opening a book and finding God? I was hooked from the first page. Lara's story is gripping and real and refreshingly honest – written with brilliance and told with grace. Even though I have not been through the same experience, I could relate to her story and the struggles that many of us face in our marriages. When I wasn't captivated by her rich language and outpouring of heart, I was captivated by the Father, and how He used this book to show me my marriage through His eyes – through His words – in accordance with His plan. Through this book He convicted me, wrapped me in grace, and reminded me "that in all things God works for the good of those who love him, who have been called according to his purpose." (Rom. 8:28) Lara found a way to take a story that was about her and make it all about God. What an awesome God we serve. I highly recommend it for any married woman, engaged woman, or woman who plans to marry.

Kelly Swanson
Motivational Speaker, Wife, Mother, High Point, North Carolina

Lara Williams teaches and reminds her readers that we are not in control, but God is, and as we accept God's sovereignty and goodness, this radically changes how we view our relationship with Him, how we view ourselves, our circumstances, and how we view and relate to others. Readers may not agree with everything Lara writes in this book. After all she illustrates how she came to a deeper understanding of God's sovereignty and goodness through her husbands' adultery, and her decision to stay married to him, despite what some others advised her to do. But whoever the reader, they most likely will be challenged, encouraged and inspired by how God worked through this woman to grow her more into the woman He wants her to be, and into a woman who came to experience less fear and true freedom.

Jane Tooher

Ministry Department, Director of the Priscilla and Aquila Centre
Moore Theological College, Sydney, Australia

To Walk or Stay is much more than a "how to" book on surviving in the aftermath of adultery. Instead of mere platitudes and practical tips, Lara Williams offers the power and beauty of God in the midst of suffering through personal and profound insights. She reveals her own inward battles as she reveals her glorious Redeemer wooing her back in intimate and heart-exposing details. As you read this book you will develop greater clarity for the life God has called you to live with Jesus, regardless of the circumstances. As a pastor, I highly recommend putting this gospel-centered book into the hands of anyone devastated by marital unfaithfulness.

Robert K. Cheong

Pastor of Care and Counseling, Sojourn Community Church, Louisville, Kentucky

To Walk or Stay

*Trusting God
through Shattered Hopes
and Suffocating Fears*

LARA WILLIAMS

CHRISTIAN
FOCUS

Lara Williams, her husband Adam, and their three children live in Greensboro, North Carolina. She holds a degree in psychology from the University of North Carolina at Chapel Hill and a Master of Divinity degree from Southeastern Baptist Theological Seminary. Her blog "To Overflowing" (tooverflowing.com) and website www.LaraWilliams.org encourage women to discover a wildly vibrant faith.

Copyright © Lara Williams 2013

paperback ISBN 978-1-78191-128-0
epub ISBN 978-1-78191-180-8
mobi ISBN 978-1-78191-186-0

10 9 8 7 6 5 4 3 2 1

Published in 2013
by
Christian Focus Publications, Ltd
Geanies House, Fearn,
Ross-shire, IV20 1TW, Scotland
www.christianfocus.com

Cover design
by
Paul Lewis

Printed by
Bell and Bain, Glasgow

CONTENTS

*I dedicate this book to my husband, Adam, who bravely
believes that our story is meant to be shared.
I love you again and again.*

Introduction

I have to confess. I often fly past a book's Introduction so I can get to the "good stuff." *I'm a bad reader*. But I pray – literally – that you read these brief words. Because some of the Truths found in this book are difficult to swallow, especially in the face of trials and the emotions that naturally follow.

With his permission, blessing and bravery, my husband's infidelity lays the backdrop for *To Walk or Stay*. But neither my husband nor his sin is the focus of this book. *For all have sinned and fall short of God's glory*. He takes ownership for what he has done in our marriage to pull us apart. I take ownership for what I've done to pull us apart. And we both believe that God wants to use our unfolding story of redemption to encourage and empower others.

The ultimate point of this book is to show you how I wrestled before my God in the midst of a devastating valley and to testify to His faithful guidance. You won't get tips on which counselor to see – though we saw many counselors. You won't get instructions on which boundaries to lay – though lines were drawn. You won't read a detailed account of my husband's transformation before His God – though he's a different man. What you will get is a dare: a dare to take God at His Word and a dare to allow His promises to affect the choices you make today.

Because here's a really amazing truth. You ready? We can't change people. *Eye-opening, I know.* You and I don't have the power to pierce hearts and transform lives. It's not our calling. But we can submit to God's "change" within us. We can be real and raw before our Lord and allow Him to radically heal our wounds. And then as He does a freedom work within us, we can even allow Him to love those who've hurt us through us...like Jesus.

Know that I've prayed for you. I've prayed that He faithfully ministers His Truth to your heart and mind. I've prayed that He would tend to any tender aches. I've prayed that you would dare to believe Him.

With eyes (imperfectly) fixed on my Lord,

Lara

1

Choosing to bind to God ... regardless

None but God can satisfy the longing of the immortal soul; as the heart was made for Him, He only can fill it.

Richard Trench
Anglican archibishop and poet, (1807-1886)

I lost my phone. It sounds so common, like something you say on an ordinary Tuesday, "I lost my phone." But *ordinary* does not describe that March night.

I stood on tired feet preparing that familiar spaghetti dinner. Steam from the boiling pasta fogged the kitchen window. Our two oldest kids sat quiet at the table, coloring. The baby gnawed on his fists while lounging contented in the bouncy seat.

I saw my husband pull into the garage. *And I felt my face scowl—loveless.* When the kids heard the door open they hollered "Daddy!" and ran to tackle. The baby looked for him with big eyes as drool ran down his chin. I avoided eye contact and gave Adam a quick side-hug for the sake of little onlookers. He did the same. Our hearts were far from one another.

I needed to make a call, so I asked to borrow his phone. Through a stuttered response, he reluctantly agreed. "What's wrong?"

I asked with accusation in my voice. "Nothing," he said sharply. I stepped into the hallway to escape the noise of three young ones vying for his attention. He followed me and hovered—nervous and fidgety—watching every button I pushed. With months of strange behavior leading to this point, my stomach immediately dropped with suspicions.

He had somewhere to be after dinner, so I prodded. "Will you leave your phone with me tonight since I can't find mine?" "No," he said defensively, "I need it." I stared at him with my jaw clenched, but he wouldn't look me in the eyes. My face got hot. The air thickened.

Yet the kids sat seemingly oblivious, protected by our God.

After we ate, he said his goodnights and goodbyes. I stayed home to do our evening routine of bath and bed. The kids were loud as usual—the happy, squealing loud. We read about David and Goliath…again. They thanked God for mommy and daddy. I kissed them, hugged them, and brought them one last sip of water. But as I closed their bedroom door, my mind began spinning with questions.

What had become of us?

Our Path to This Point

For years I had feasted upon lies about love. My college life had left deep wounds in my spirit. Though God had freed me from pits of addiction and promiscuity long before Adam and I ever met, I still had tender places that needed His healing touch. I had bought into the Hollywood falsities that pictured true love with happily-ever-after dreams. Even while I studied at seminary,

I imagined a husband who would eagerly serve me like Christ. I hoped he would gaze into my eyes while detailing my exquisite beauty. *You're laughing.* We met and married with that mindset still plaguing my heart.

Adam also entered marriage deceived. Sexual distortions and addictions marked his past. Our fallen world taught him from an early age that love equaled sex. So to him, wedding bells meant sexual euphoria.

We started building walls between us in the early days of marriage. We each laid brick after brick as unspoken, unmet expectations pulled us apart. And as the wall between us grew higher and wider, something in me started questioning Christ's teachings regarding love. The selfless love of my Lord felt unattainable and possibly untrue.

Initially I asked what many young wives ask of God, "Will You please change this man?! Please!" But the Lord seemed silent and distant. And slowly over time my heart calloused towards my man. Criticisms occupied my mind. Doubts and regret consumed me. This seminary girl, raised preacher's daughter, started to quietly beg God for a way out of my marriage.

Little did I know, my "way out" would mean my own transformation through a valley of brokenness.

Five years and two children into our marriage, my prayers began to change. I was tired of the same charade. I wanted the abundance and victory, joy and peace that Christ died to give me. I wanted the things promised in Scripture—the things I taught as Truth to other women. And I wanted them regardless of my circumstance. So by His grace I finally humbled myself and said,

"Father, if you aren't going to change my man, then change me. Change me." And a year later on that March night, God began to break me.

That March Night

Adam headed straight to the shower when he got home on that cool March night. I snuck into the bathroom, searching for his phone. I needed my sister's opinion. With knots in the pit of my stomach, I called her and choked out six words I never thought I'd say, "I think he might be cheating." Holding back her protective, sisterly anger, she gave me wise counsel and then promised to pray.

The night was long. I didn't have the courage to confront him, so I wallowed in quiet despair. Fears interrupted my sleep. Questions consumed my mind. Contempt over the unknown stirred in my spirit. Yet my stranger-of-a-man slept sound beside me.

The next morning he left for work as usual. I stayed home with the kids trying to be engaged in everyday life as a mommy. *But the clock ticks slowly when a mind races.* Once my young ones laid down for an afternoon nap, I went searching for evidence. I contemplated Adam's patterns over recent months and begged God for clarity. I wanted the facts regardless of the possible pain.

Layer by layer God pulled back the veil and opened my eyes to the betrayal. And I broke. I buried my face into our cold, red leather couch, nauseous with the details. I laid there and sobbed over the mess of our lives.

As my kids awoke from their nap, I dried my worn eyes and forced a smile. We grabbed my niece's present and left for her first birthday celebration. The paradox felt awkward. Kids laughed innocently while all I could feel was the throb of an open gash in my chest.

I had no idea that even in those early moments of soul-chaos, the enemies of darkness were losing the death grip they held on our home. The Almighty had launched an all-out assault on the strong-holds suffocating our family. And walls were going to crumble.

In the weeks that followed, I battled raw emotions. I wrestled with tough questions. I wanted to honor my Lord. I did. But the ache weighed down so strong that I honestly just wanted to be released from my vows. Nightmares replaced my once-peaceful sleep. My husband's voice made me cringe. I needed space. And time.

I needed Truth.

The Lord allowed me time to grieve. For I suppose a death had occurred—a death of the old to make way for the new. But in the midst of that grief God spoke, and by His grace I listened.

The Promise that Came Through Binding

I had a choice. I could've walked. I could've quit. I could've packed up the kids and run away. In fact my emotions screamed at me to leave. But deep down where God's Spirit stirs, He prompted me towards something different—something radically foreign.

I didn't hear Him audibly, but I clearly sensed Him saying, "Lara, you can go. You can walk. I will always be with you. But, if you choose to leave, you will miss My ultimate blessing." The thought made me sick. I questioned Him with bitterness of heart, "Don't you see what this man has done? Don't you care that I am broken?"

But His ways are infinitely beyond ours.

In my own self, I was weak. The thought of staying caused my knees to buckle. My youngest was three months old when the madness settled in. Needless to say, I wasn't just emotionally weary from the breaking. I was physically weary from the lack of sleep. The Lord knew I needed a word of hope.

I turned to that often-quoted passage in Isaiah where he proclaimed, "They who wait on the Lord shall renew their strength; they shall mount up with wings like eagles; they shall run and not be weary; they shall walk and not faint."[1] And though the thought of soaring and running sounded glorious, it seemed impossible. I dug further into the passage, trying to figure out exactly what He wanted me to do.

Wait. To this microwave-society girl, that four-letter word made me cringe. But I discovered something exciting when I peeled back the layers on the word "wait." In fact, the word *wait* didn't mean to wait. The word literally meant "to bind together; this word stresses the straining of the mind in a certain direction with an expectant attitude."[2]

He wasn't calling me to sit around and eat chocolate while waiting. *Though that was a tempting choice.* He was calling me to bind to Him. He was calling me to strain my mind towards His promises, expecting that He would indeed be faithful.

From that Isaiah text, He promised to renew my strength if I bound myself to Him. I dissected the text even further to discover that He didn't want to revive my old, dead, human strength. He

---

1   Isaiah 40:31.

2   Strong, James, and John R. Kohlenberger III. "Wait." *The New Strong's Expanded Exhaustive Concordance of the Bible*. Nashville: Thomas Nelson Publishers, 2001 (p. 245, H6960).

promised to give me *His* strength. An exchange would occur. *Then* I would be prepared for flight. Like an eagle that soars, I would ride *His* currents without having to flap my tired wings. He would carry me over the valley.

It sounded good. But part of me wondered if it was true. In the weeks to come I fervently bound myself to Him. I sought after my Lord through His Word and spent extended time in prayer. I didn't know what to do, or how to be, but I knew I needed His direction. And in the midst of my cluttered living room—cluttered with toys and laundry and fears—this God who spoke worlds into existence bent down and spoke a word of promise to me.

I'm not sure how I got there. I don't typically cozy up on the couch to read the book of Joel on a rainy day. But He spoke a promise from its pages: "I will restore to you the years that the swarming locust has eaten...You shall eat in plenty and be satisfied, and praise the name of the Lord your God, who has dealt wondrously with you."[3]

As I read Joel's words, penned thousands of years prior by this prophet to Israel, my God spoke to me. He spoke to this girl in the twenty-first century with a broken heart and a broken home. And I cried tears of joy, tears of pain, even tears of disbelief.

At first I didn't want to accept the word. My heart was crushed. I knew that this would be a slow walk—a crawl—of faith. After some hesitation, I finally took the outstretched hand of my God, clung to the promise from His Word, and said a reluctant "yes" to Him. I didn't know how restoration would look. But He said the years would be restored, so by His grace I chose to believe Him. I chose to stay in our marriage in spite of how I felt.

---

3   Joel 2:25-26.

Our One Weapon

To think that God would speak through His Word to those seeking His face humbles me. His Word breathes.[4] If we are willing to look and listen, it meets us in the fires of life and soothes the burn on an intimate level. Through His Word He promises, prophecies and penetrates even the hardest of hearts. Through it He guides even through the darkest of valleys – through *whatever* valley we find ourselves treading.

I haven't always been convinced of the value of God's Word. I grew up as the stereotypical, rebellious Southern Baptist preacher's kid. Though I accepted Jesus at age nine, by high school I was the wild child. I attended nearly every church event and could brush on an innocent smile with ease. But beneath the compliant exterior I lied, cheated, and pulled others down with me. My daddy preached the Bible as Truth, but I rejected the possibility that it could affect my moments.

By age eighteen, I left for college self-focused and self-destructive. My dad's quick death during my freshman year sent me spiraling out of control. Instead of turning to God, I ran fast and hard in the opposite direction.

Thankfully, three years before meeting Adam, the Lord had brought me to my knees. After a near-death experience, I finally began to seek the God from my childhood. *Was His face as I remembered*? My Bible had grown dusty, tucked away on that college bookshelf. But as I opened its pages, His Word touched me afresh. It came alive. And I bowed before Him, confessing my rebellion and resting in His cleansing.

---

4   Hebrews 4:12.

In the months to follow, I fell deeply in love with my Lord and His Word. It quenched my soul-thirst. His Truth pierced to the division of my soul and spirit.[5] That's when He called me to seminary. I remember telling my mom as I packed, "Well, I guess I just need my Bible. And maybe some clothes." I became convinced. *Convicted.*

His Word is alive.

It is both reliable and authoritative.[6] He has proven its faithfulness over and over in my own little life. Paul describes the Word as our sword in this fight for faith. We are in the midst of a spiritual battle. "[We wrestle] against principalities, against powers, against the rulers of the darkness of this age, against spiritual hosts of wickedness in the heavenly places."[7] Without our sword sharp and ready, we will fall prey to the enemy's lies.

I fall prey to the enemy's lies.

War-talk isn't my thing. I am a girl. I like to paint my toenails. I like everyone to get along and be kind. I want peace and quiet. But I have two young boys who turn everything into a weapon. They continually search for the "bad guy" so they can destroy him with their plastic swords. They growl with contorted faces, ready to attack their victim—often their *older* sister. And I stare and pray that I might understand their warrior hearts.

Whether we like war-talk or not, we're in the midst of a battle. And it isn't fluffy and pretty. Peter describes the enemy as a lion

---

5   Hebrews 4:12.

6   A few resources that defend the authenticity of the Bible include: Phillip E. Johnson's *Reason in the Balance*; Ronald H. Nash's *Is Jesus the Only Savior?* and *Faith and Reason*; Lee Strobel's *The Case for Christ*; J. P. Moreland's *Love Your God With All Your Mind*; and *When Critics Ask*, by Norman Geisler and Thomas Howe.

7   Ephesians 6:12, NKJV.

seeking whom he may devour.[8] He prowls and pursues. He tempts and twists. He knows our weaknesses and attacks relentlessly— though within the boundaries our Father sets for His children.

Because of *whom* we are fighting against, we have to clothe ourselves with the armor that will actually protect. In those early years of marriage, I wasn't battling my man. It felt like I was battling my man, but ultimately I battled against an enemy out to destroy our home.

The sword of the Spirit—the Word of God—is our only offensive weapon. Unless we marinate in the Word, sharpening our swords, we will fall susceptible to the lies of the enemy. And he will lie. He is the father of lies. He lies to me continually. He even lied to Jesus.

After forty days of fasting and prayer in the wilderness, the enemy met Jesus with ferocious temptation.[9] Jesus responded to each of the enemy's lies with the truth of Scripture, declaring with absolute conviction, "It is written." *It is written.* In order to identify lies, we have to know Truth. We must know what He said in the Scriptures in order to say with assurance, "It is written."

Once He shined His light into our home, the enemy began to bombard me with lies. He spoke slight distortions while playing on my raw emotions. He whispered confidently, "This is over. There is no hope. God wants you happy. You have rights. It's all Adam's fault. You deserve better." At times I fell prey. I went down into that pit of hopeless despair. But my Lord would faithfully remind me of His truths, and, only by His grace, I chose

---

8   1 Peter 5:8.

9   See Luke 4:1-13.

to grip my sword tight and battle the enemy with the only weapon mighty in God for casting down distortion.

With the aim of following my Lord's lead, I began responding to the enemy boldly with the promises of my God. *With God all things are possible.*[10] *Love hopes.*[11] *He is sovereign so He is working.*[12] *He has me here with purpose, for my good and His ultimate glory. He will never forsake me.*[13] *He has placed a hedge around me.*[14] I preached His Truth to my soul. I wrote His promises on note cards. I often struggled to believe Him, but in spite of my feelings, I bound myself to His Word.

The Ultimate Blessing

Early in marriage I had thought that the greatest blessing would be for my man to change. But in actuality, the greatest blessing came when I found myself in that inner room of intimacy with God. When I processed the pain with the Lover of my soul, I experienced a joy that this world couldn't steal. Through the valley of brokenness I learned that true blessing rises as I bind to my God regardless of circumstance.

I chose to stay, but it wasn't a heroic choice. It was one that God led me to make; and one I made only by His strength. In that staying, He faithfully restored in more ways than I could have ever imagined.

This book isn't a prescription. If anything, it's a testimony of God's faithfulness through a personal season of brokenness. If anything, it's a dare to take Him at His Word.

---

10   Matthew 19:26.

11   1 Corinthians 13:7.

12   Matthew 10:29.

13   Deuteronomy 31:6.

14   Psalm 139:5.

SMALL GROUP DISCUSSION

- Read Psalm 119:105-108, John 8:31-32, and Hebrews 4:12.

- What does God promise in relation to His Word?

- How do His promises challenge your belief system?

- How can you choose to bind to the Lord in the day-to-day, regardless of your feelings?

DIGGING DEEPER

Sometimes worry or fear just feels right. Doesn't it? A circumstance enters our mundane Tuesday and we find ourselves riding that emotional roller-coaster. Our hearts dance with anxiety or revenge, all the while desperate to find a solid place upon which to stand. Thankfully, our God gave us His sweet Word.

Read Jeremiah 17:5-10, then answer the following questions to determine why our hearts are so needy for His renewing touch.

The word "cursed" means "detestable." Whenever God declares something as "detestable," then it's time to listen up. What does He declare "detestable"? (v. 5)

How does "trusting in man" (or circumstance) play out in our everyday lives? What does it look like?

He describes the inner man as a desert shrub. What adjectives describe a desert shrub?

When I hear the word "wilderness" my mind automatically travels back in time to the forty years that God's people walked in the desert. Read Deuteronomy 1:19-46. Why did the Israelites remain in the wilderness for forty years?

We live under His blessing when we believe in the Lord—when we put our hope in His faithful character. What does it look like to practically hope in the Lord rather than in mankind or circumstance?

Why is it that we do not need to fear or be anxious, even when the fiery trials of life come our way? (Jer. 17:8)

What verses of Scripture can you think of to aid in the battle against fear and anxiety?

He promises that we can indeed bear fruit even in the midst of a drought. Read Galatians 5:22. What is the fruit of the Spirit that we can yield regardless of our circumstance?

Returning to the Jeremiah text, how does God describe the heart in vv. 9-10?

Blessing and cursing flow from the state of the heart. If our inner man is trusting in, resting in, and believing God, then blessing will flow—fruit will burst forth. But if our inner man is depending on things or people of this world to fulfill our deepest cravings, then we live under the curse. How would you describe your own heart these days?

2

Laying down my need to control

God had one Son on earth without sin, but never one without suffering.

Augustine

also known as St. Augustine, Bishop of Hippo Regius, theologian and philosopher,
(A.D. 354-430)

God spoke a promise of restoration, but I still battled strong emotions. Life had changed overnight. Our house looked the same. Our kids looked the same. But every single thing had changed. Though God had prepared me to some extent, the betrayal crushed me. The rejection caused deep insecurities to surface. The details of my husband's rebellion plagued me. And I felt as if I had no say—no control—over my circumstance. *Which is exactly where He wanted me to be.*

Up until then, I thought I controlled my life. I had boxes in my mind where I neatly placed people and situations, defining how life should behave. The labels on the outside explained the contents. And the lids stayed tightly closed.

On one box I scribbled "husband." On another it said "kids." On a third I wrote "health." A big box in the corner said "God." I stacked them in alphabetical order. And as long as the contents obeyed my rules and stayed in their labeled boxes, everything ran smoothly. My soul rested. But when the contents slipped out over the edge of the box, when it felt as if I lost control over my circumstance, a crisis took place within me. *A crisis now took place within me.*

When I Started Having Control Issues

I started collecting boxes early in life. As the obedient first-born who didn't get many spankings, I controlled my world by being good. I knew what to expect when I behaved. So I labeled my boxes and set one basic rule: obedience will bring tangible blessing.

But in high school I changed my mind, concluding that I *didn't* actually have the control; my parents did. That's when I bucked the system, becoming that prodigal preacher's kid, determined to be the one in control. When my dad died, I realized that I had *zero* control. I couldn't help him or stop the sickness. As if mirroring my soul-anguish, I lost all outward control and gave into fleshly cravings. No boxes, only a scattered mess.

Until He grabbed me.

When He woke me from those rebellious years, changing me from the inside out, I began to feel some semblance of control again. And I started arranging my boxes. But these were good, Christian boxes—the right kind that supposedly honored my Lord. I defined what my husband would do, how my kids would behave, and what this God would allow. In essence, I fed the lie that promised "nice and neat" if I was "good and obedient."

Though at seminary I studied the words of Jesus that talked about suffering and I read of martyrs who died for the faith, part of me didn't believe. Part of me thought that blessing meant ease of days and picture perfect.

After my husband and I got married I realized that he wouldn't stay in my husband-box. Life wasn't going as planned. He didn't want to do what I thought he should do. He didn't smile and say "thanks" when I gave godly "advice" on how he should act or what he should say. And he didn't offer to rub my feet every night—a very basic prerequisite to the godly man. *Didn't he get that memo?*

I wanted him to change. I suggested books for him to read and bought different clothes for him to wear. I tried to coax him with my words in efforts to win his affection—in efforts to control him.

In essence, I behaved out of the curse upon Eve. Remember her? She and Adam were the first people, created and blessed by God. They walked intimately with Him until they chose to disobey His one boundary—the boundary He set out of love. Then they blamed one another for their rebellion. *Just like I do.* For years I thought, "If only my husband would get it together, then I could be a contented wife." Blame.

God disciplined them both, along with the enemy, saying to Eve, "Your desire shall be for your husband and he shall rule over you."[1] He didn't speak a word of blessing. He spoke discipline. For the generations to follow, wives everywhere would battle this

---

1   Genesis 3:16b.

desire for our men—more specifically the desire to *control* our men.

In this flesh of mine, I tried to control him. I wanted good things for him mainly because I wanted good things for me. I wanted to be in control. I wanted him to stay in my husband-box.

Then there was my God-box. It was bigger than my husband-box but still had walls and rules. With His Word as my defense, I quietly planned my way out of our marriage should infidelity ever occur—willing to walk through adultery if it meant my freedom. I defined my God and told Him how things would work. *Nice and neat.*

But when God spoke those words of restoration from the book of Joel, He challenged me. I couldn't believe He would expect me to stay, or dare even ask. I couldn't reconcile His call with my expectations. And my God-box exploded. The realization that I wasn't in control left me feeling bare and exposed all over again—just like after my dad died.

By His grace, I didn't run as I had in college. Instead, I wrestled with Him while angry and bitter. I asked tough questions about divorce and sex and love. I pressed more deeply into Him than I ever had before. And He redefined me. He redefined *Himself* to me.

Even the Sparrows

When faced with difficulties we have choice as to where we begin. We can begin with the trial and define God through the lens of circumstance, or we can begin with God and define the trial through the lens of His revealed character. The choice is ours. If we begin with the circumstance, we will inevitably end up with an erroneous view of the Lord. But if we begin with Him, strength can rise.

I had to begin with God. Choosing to define Him through the lens of circumstance left me feeling hopeless. So He led me to three short verses that hold profound implications. These truths gave me a hope upon which to stand. I rediscovered them in the book of Matthew.

Jesus teaches that not one sparrow falls to the ground apart from the Father's will. That speaks of His sovereignty. Nothing catches Him off guard. Nothing falls outside of His realm of control—not even the dying of a bird. *Not even the betrayal of a spouse?*

Jesus then tells that the Father numbers the very hairs of my head—even the gray ones that I vainly try to cover up. He knows me perfectly and intimately. He sees my sitting and my going. He gets every joke I tell and knows the intent of my heart, even when no one else does. I'm completely known by Him, down to my strands of hair.[2]

Jesus concludes, "Do not fear therefore; you are of more value than many sparrows."[3] *Do not fear*. He says we need not fear because our individual value exceeds that of many sparrows.

But I did fear. For a while, fear debilitated my faith. Fear strangled all hope. I feared being alone. Yet I feared being with a man

---

2   See Psalm 139.

3   Matthew 10:29-31, NKJV.

who betrayed my trust. I feared what others would think. I feared the effects on my kids. Yet Jesus says "Do not fear" for one reason and one reason alone: God the Father *is* in control. *He's in control.* He numbers the birds of the air, determining when each will fall to the ground. And He is sovereign over my today.

I stood there with fear for a while. I weighed Jesus' words next to my shattered home. I questioned whether my devastation truly fell under the category of "Fear not." And again I bound myself to His promises. He even—gently—convicted me that with every coddled fear, I looked my God in the face and said, "I don't believe that You have this thing under control. I don't trust You."

I wanted to cast out the fear. I *wanted* to. So I searched His Word for the *how*. I knew fear would come as a natural response to changes in life, so I wanted to know how to fight it. It was then that John's words came alive: "There is no fear in love; but perfect love casts out fear, because fear involves torment. But he who fears has not been made perfect in love."[4]

Perfect love casts out fear. Only my God gives perfect love. But in the midst of fears and *un*control, I couldn't grasp His perfect love. The valley seemed to trump His promise.

But I could choose to believe Him.

Most times in opposition to my feelings, I began choosing to believe that His love motivated the things He had allowed into my life—even this excruciating valley. Over time, He taught me how to bring those fearful thoughts captive to truth. He taught me how to engage the battle against the lies that caused the fear to

---

4   1 John 4:18, NKJV.

arise.[5] As I believed His love to be over me, surrounding me, and in me, the fear had to flee.

When my home and marriage seemed unrecognizable, He said, "Do not fear." When the sting of betrayal hurt deep, He responded, "Do not fear." As His child, I had not slipped off His radar. He saw me. I didn't need to fear and clamor for control because my God was present and active and reigning.

Though my feelings tempted disbelief at times, He set my feet on a new course. I was going to dare to believe that my God had this thing under His control.

Why the Valleys
This side of Christ's return, valleys will come. Some valleys will knock us clear to the ground with their unpredictability. Others will just trip us up, leaving dust on our shoes. Regardless of the degree, they will come. But I'm convinced that He remains in complete control.

He is the omnipotent Almighty One. Slowly I've come to believe that He allows every single valley in the life of His children out of His love. He allowed my own personal breaking out of love. He allowed the pain partly to free me from my selfish agenda. He allowed the stripping away as a vehicle to build my faith in His absolute sufficiency. Because when everything else vanished, I depended more fiercely. I believed more radically.

I'm always inspired by the story of Job. Though not the most encouraging read at the outset, the happenings with Job enlighten

---

5   In Chapter Four I give practical tips on taking our thoughts captive to truth.

us to the ways of our God. We see that God offered up Job—the most righteous man in the land—to be sifted by the enemy. *God offered him to Satan.*[6] And He only set one boundary: the enemy could not kill Job.

How could this be good?

How could this be love?

Job experienced devastating trial. He lost everyone he loved—except his not-so-tender wife. He lost everything he had worked to gain. He lost his health. He lived through excruciating pain—physically, emotionally and spiritually. Yet God allowed every aspect of the ache. And when we marry His sovereignty with His pursuing love, I have to believe that He allowed every aspect with purpose.

Through the pain, God revealed Himself to Job. Through the devastation, God opened his eyes. Through the suffering, God exposed His holy nature. Through the trials, Job came face-to-face with His Maker and finally responded, "I have heard You by the hearing of the ear, but now my eye sees You. Therefore I abhor myself, and repent in dust and ashes."[7]

When Job saw God as He truly is—completely beyond us in power and purpose—he responded with great humility. And in the end, Job completely trusted his God. And God restored Job and all his losses. In fact, He blessed Job's latter days even more than his first.[8] He allowed the suffering to grow Job's faith and prune his character. He ultimately allowed it for Job's good and for God's great glory.

---

6   Job 1:6-12.

7   Job 42:5-6, NKJV.

8   Job 42:10-17.

Trials will come. Hopefully not as devastating as those of Job, but this side of Jesus they *will* come. And in Christ, we can do more than just survive. According to His Word, it's possible to count these trials as joy. "Count it all joy, my brothers, when you meet trials of various kinds, for you know that the testing of your faith produces steadfastness. And let steadfastness have its full effect, that you may be perfect and complete, lacking in nothing."[9]

James implies that the joy erupting from an enduring faith is greater than the pain brought on by the momentary trial. He isn't foolishly teaching us to deny the pain. Trials burn, sometimes to an excruciating degree. But He calls us to trust that suffering can birth a refined faith that has the potential to bring deeply satisfying joy. Our calling is to count it so. He beckons us to believe.

Not even a sparrow falls to the ground apart from the Father's will.

The words of my God's absolute sovereignty infused hope in me. My marriage lay as a pile of ruins, but my God was in control. My heavenly Daddy considered me greatly valuable. And everything that entered my life somehow, some way, had purpose. My heart needed me to believe.

Freedom That Comes With Release
As my faith in His sovereign control grew, my soul found unimaginable freedom. I didn't need to contend for control. I didn't need to impose false boundaries on my God. I didn't need to set the agenda.

---

9   James 1:2-4.

The valley was still dark ahead of me and the rocky ground cut the soles of my feet, but as His Spirit empowered me to surrender to Him—in spite of my feelings—God's peace overwhelmed. A rest unexplainable arose in my spirit as I chose to believe His sovereignty and trust His love.

This newfound freedom to trust Him also came with a freedom to love my man without expectation. Though not without heart struggle, I slowly released him. I set him free from my rules and let him be his own man before a holy God. I got out of the way and determined to set my gaze on my Lord, trusting Him to work restoration into our reality. Trusting Him to work in my husband's heart, in *His* time and in *His* way.

I didn't do it perfectly. I struggled with my thoughts and wrestled with forgiveness. But in time, I stopped maneuvering and contriving. I stopped depending on my husband for lasting joy. I let him go and asked my God to simply love, forgive and glorify Himself through me. The Lord faithfully revealed when I reached down to pick up the reins. And I would lay them down again. *And again.*

It took the brokenness for me to realize that I can't control my circumstance. I can't control those beside me. I can't control my God. But I can bring myself into submission to His will. I can allow Him to transform me through this pain. I can lay myself before Him and ask that He love others through me...unconditionally.

SMALL GROUP DISCUSSION

• How have you seen the "desire to control" play out in your own life?

• How have you wrestled with God's sovereignty over the happenings in your own life?

• What does believing Him sovereign stir up in your own spirit?

DIGGING DEEPER

We crave the façade of control. We find comfort in thinking that our efforts determine our "fate." But we live in a fallen world. Disease, sin and hurt lace the edges of life. If we can bury His eternal truth deep down and believe what He declares, then the trials lose some of their debilitating power over us. So let's dig in.

Read James 1:2-8. *Joy*. He says to count it all joy when we fall into various trials. The word *joy* in this text means "calm delight; or gladness." Calm delight? Gladness?

The word translated "trials" in verse 2 is the same Greek word translated as "temptation" in verse 12. The word means "a putting to proof; trial with a beneficial purpose or effect; divinely permitted or sent."[10] Read that definition again, slow and steady. In your own words, gleaning from the definitions given above, rewrite verse 2.

What are some of the various trials that you have walked (or are currently walking) through?

In looking at this text and thinking on other texts you already have in your heart, how can believers possibly count it all joy when we fall into these various trials? What perspective does James encourage us to keep?

Do you have any "hang-ups" or places of confusion with the idea of counting it all joy even amidst difficult happenings? If so, what are they?

When faced with various trials we desperately need God's vision. He reigns above and beyond the circumstance. He allowed it with purpose, not apart from His great love. We need His view that we might

---

10   Strong, "Temptation" (p. 196, G3986).

obey, *and live.* If you are currently facing a trial—a testing of your faith—how can you actively seek His wisdom in faith?

Read James 1:12. What do we receive when we endure the trials of life?

This type of crown was a symbol of triumph for the person who won the race. We are running a race of faith in this life. The victory comes when we trust that He is in complete control, only allowing that which will be for our ultimate good and His ultimate glory.

Take some time to write out your thoughts and prayer to our Lord. Be real. Be raw. Then allow His Truth to invade and rain down. He promises renewed strength for those who bind to Him. What specific verses encourage your spirit?

3

He exposed my thoughts

Habits of thought are not less tyrannical than other habits, and a time comes when return is impossible, even to the strongest will.

Alexander Vinet
Swiss critic and theologian, (1797-1847)

Though it didn't come without soul-opposition, I got to the place where I accepted God's sovereignty over our trial. I began trusting His love as the motivator. I chose to believe that He had purpose in this pain and that He would fulfill His promises. And all of those choices brought hope. But when a friend gently suggested that maybe God wanted to change *me* through the valley, I got a little gruff. I felt my upper lip do that thing it does when I get disgusted. *Excuse me? I'm not the one that needs fixing.*

But her words stuck with me. Though at first I denied any part in our plight, I couldn't shake the possibility that maybe I did have a couple of areas that needed slight tweaking. *Just a couple. Slight tweaking.* At the very least, I didn't want to walk this road again. If I had something that needed purging, I wanted it gone. So I figured I should ask His opinion. He definitely had an opinion.

He prompted me to consider my thought life. And the discovery grieved me.

41

One afternoon I sat with a pen in hand and my journal open. I asked Him to show me every single thought I was thinking, especially about my man. "I'm ready," I said. Then, one-by-one I wrote them down. And one-by-one I grew heavier with conviction. It was as if God lifted the scales from my eyes. He gave me vision to see my thoughts. And to be honest, they sickened me. I taught in the church. I claimed to love God and love my family. But I tore my own husband apart in my mind. That wasn't love.

I could hold my tongue. Growing up an obedient little girl taught me well. But negativity towards my husband consumed my thoughts. I criticized his weaknesses and belittled his efforts. From the early days of our marriage, I had regretted saying "yes" to the proposal and wanted a way out. Though I outwardly appeared to be a blessing—preparing his meals, washing his clothes, raising our kids—inwardly I held contempt towards him. And my meditations fueled the strife between us.

Broken, I repented. I asked my Lord to forgive me. I asked Him to transform this part of me. I needed my mind to be free from the divisiveness. *Our marriage needed my mind to be free from the divisiveness*. The Lord faithfully showed up.

Thinking What I Feel

He began exposing my thought patterns. Most of my thoughts were feelings-based. If I felt hurt, I thought on that hurt. If I experienced a disappointment, I continually rehashed it in my mind. If my man upset me, I criticized him for days. My feelings fueled my thoughts. And my mind was a dishonorable mess.

Feeling-based thoughts *feel* right. They affirm what our heart experiences. And though feelings are very real, I've learned that they

42

are not a reliable place upon which to stand. Jeremiah unashamedly describes the heart as "deceitful...and desperately sick."[1] My own heart had deceived me. I had allowed my mind to follow my deceitful heart and it played into the destruction of my home. I'm not claiming full responsibility for the mess in which we found ourselves, we each have to stand individually before our Maker. But I fully believe that my thought life played into the rebellion of my man.

It makes sense. God said, "[A man and his wife] become one flesh."[2] My man and I were one. My thoughts affected him. Though I mostly guarded my mouth, my attitude portrayed hatred. My general tone degraded him. My mindset rarely lifted him or helped him or blessed him. And he sensed it.

I allowed my thoughts to wander, and the trail led to dissatisfaction and disillusionment. I lacked joy and peace. I believed lies and chained myself with bitterness. For when we follow after our slippery feelings, we do what we once swore against. We react and flare up. We subject ourselves to lies.

That's exactly what I had done.

Once I got back up from the blow to my pride, I decided that I wanted more than my opinion or feelings. I wanted a transformed mind. I desired to obey and think on things that were true, noble, just, pure and lovely instead of the poison that I had feasted upon for years.[3] So, I gave my mind to Him and told Him to have His way: "Just be gentle."

---

1   Jeremiah 17:9.

2   Genesis 2:24.

3   Philippians 4:8.

Things Don't Change By Accident

Everything begins with a thought. Every feeling, every action, and every belief originates in the mind. And we're continually thinking. So I knew that the battle to transform my mind would take diligence. It wouldn't happen by accident. It wouldn't happen if I coasted. I had to fight for the sound mind Christ died to give me.[4] *The same sound mind He died to give you.*

Paul teaches believers that we have the weapons mighty in God for bringing every thought captive to obedience.[5] The idea that we need to take something captive presupposes a battle. This was going to be war. But, according to Scripture, I had weapons that empowered me to bring every bitter thought, every angry thought, every lustful thought and every envious thought into obedience. And my one offensive weapon was His Word.

According to His Word I had choice. I could *choose* what would captivate my mind. He didn't say the angry thoughts wouldn't come; or that the "justifiable" feelings wouldn't surface. I'm convinced that as long as we wrestle against this flesh, they will arise. But, in Him, I had choice. Victory meant moment-by-moment choice. And I wanted to choose His blessing.

To choose His blessing I had to raise the sword of His Word. I had to remove it from its sheath and grip the handle tight. I had to meditate on His Truths—memorizing verses that met me in my own struggles.

---

4   2 Timothy 1:7 NKJV.

5   See 2 Corinthians 10:3-6.

Choosing on Monday, and then on Tuesday

One by one, I examined my list of thoughts and discovered that I often focused on my man's weaknesses. I tore him down in places where he already felt defeated, and then I left him there without any thought of tending to him. But the Lord revealed that my husband, first and foremost, was my brother in Christ. Some of his choices had hurt me, but I had hurt him. We were both in process. And true love would intercede. True love would be his helper.

When thoughts of his weaknesses arose, instead of tearing him down, I learned to break away to a quiet place and pray for him. *That's what I want others to do for me.* I asked God to give him victory over his struggles. I asked Him to free my man from things that hindered the flow of joy. I learned to stand in the gap, beginning with a single thought.

I found that when I chose intercession over degradation, my heart softened towards him. As I prayed for him, my vision changed. I saw him with God's eyes rather than my own. Compassion for him stirred. And I longed for him to experience true freedom over those places that tripped him up. It wasn't easy. *At times it still isn't easy.* My emotions often put up a fight, but choosing intercession proved to be the most fruitful choice. We always have the choice to pray for those who've hurt us rather than tear them down. It's what Jesus did.

I also realized that I continually relived past wounds. Things had happened. He had deeply hurt me. And my feelings made it difficult to breathe at times. That was the reality. But dwelling on the

45

pain left me defeated and depressed. Those thought patterns stole the promised joy of salvation.[6] The time had come to focus upon the character of my Healer instead of the ache.

When past hurts came to mind, tempting me to dwell, I learned to take those thoughts to Him. He graciously allowed me to pour out the pain at His feet but He also mended my soul with His Truth. He washed the pain with His promises. I would speak aspects of His character out loud, often through the tears. *You allowed that with purpose. You are always good. You are always love. You hear my cries. You heal my wounds. I trust You.* I clung to the restoration promises from the book of Joel that He had faithfully spoken, repeating and memorizing them. I chose to sing songs of praise instead of reliving places of despair. And over time, I lingered less in the past and more in my today.

But my man's weaknesses and past wounds weren't the only destructive thoughts on my list. *I'm telling you. Serious issues.* I also entertained my share of lies. I thought on lies regarding our marriage, believing it all to be hopeless and impossible to redeem. I pondered lies about my God, denying His ability to transform and overlooking His disdain of my pride. I even believed lies about myself, as if I had it all together and my husband was the only problem.

My mind didn't reflect my identity as a new creation in Christ. *A Master's in Divinity meant nothing if the truths of Scripture didn't affect my thought life.* Instead, I reflected one who still fed the flesh with all of its deceptions.

---

6   Psalm 51:12.

Paul says for us as believers not to walk like the world in the "futility of their minds."[7] Instead, the abundant life arises when we "put off your old self, which belongs to your former manner of life and is corrupt through deceitful desires, and...be renewed in the spirit of your minds, and...put on the new self, created after the likeness of God in true righteousness and holiness."[8] Put off. Put on.

This old, dead way of thinking had to go. For God to be glorified in and through me, this transformation had to stick. And by His great grace, I learned a new way. Please don't hear me say this was uncomplicated or trouble-free. It was hard. Learning a new bent with my thought life came with great struggle. I wrestled against tough emotions. But instead of being a wife that internally condemned this man, I wanted to be a wife that blessed him, even with my thoughts. I'm fully convinced that holding my tongue wasn't enough. God's plan includes complete freedom for us, beginning in our thought lives.

Disciplined in Love

Out of His love, my gracious God had corrected me. He desired freedom for my thought life, so He revealed my bent. The writer of Hebrews teaches that God disciplines His own in order that we may partake of His holiness, yielding the peaceable fruit of righteousness.[9] Imagine. We can partake of His holiness as a result of His discipline. As He sheds needful things from us, the peaceable fruit of righteousness grows. That humbles me.

---

7   Ephesians 4:17.

8   Ephesians 4:22-24.

9   Hebrews 12:10-11.

47

Now that I'm slowly stepping out of the foggy valley, I can see that my God disciplined me through that pain—for my good and His glory. He desired better things for me and better things for my home. He knew the distortion that bound my mind. Christ died to give the best things—freedom things. To experience His best, my mind needed His touch.

Effects of a Transformed Mind

The changes in my thought life brought great changes in our home. I became less feelings-led and more Spirit-led. My countenance reflected the hope and peace that was beginning to characterize my soul. And my words more often imparted grace than corruption, because as we meditate on true things, true things then flow from our lips. [10]

I failed often. *I still fail.* I still have to consciously choose true thoughts throughout the moments of daily life. When I sense a bad attitude in myself, I pray for Him to reveal my heart meditations. And then, one-by-one, I replace those thoughts with true things.

He changed me. He transformed my mind. He transformed my life.

Revive Us

Revival in our world begins with revival in our homes. And revival in our homes begins with revival in our individual hearts and minds. Regardless of what marks our days, whether marital struggles or health concerns, we have a choice as to what

---

10   Ephesians 4:29.

captivates our minds. He gives us weapons mighty in Him for bringing every single thought captive to obedience. His Word is our sword.

As we meditate on God's Word rather than our volatile feelings, hope arises. As we choose to ponder the Truth of His character rather than our fleeting circumstance, peace falls. He gives us this one life, these few days. May we not waste them with futile thinking.

SMALL GROUP DISCUSSION

- Do you find your thoughts are more feelings-led or Spirit-led? Discuss.

- Give an example of how your thought life has affected your attitude, either positively or negatively.

- What one action step can you take this week in taking your thoughts captive to truth?

| Digging Deeper |

The battle for the mind will be continual. If we do not engage the fight, then false thinking will take us prisoner, in turn stealing the victory Christ died to give us. *All of this war-talk makes me feel like painting my face and growling like my warrior boys.*

Read Colossians 3:1-17 and then note who we are in Christ as described in the text. (e.g. raised with Him, v. 1)

Looking at the same passage, what are we empowered to do considering our identity in Christ? (e.g. seek those things which are above, v. 1)

It is because of our identity *in Him* that we are enabled to take captive our thoughts. Compare and contrast the old man versus the new man. Be specific. Circle which adjectives more often characterize your own thought life.

In this passage Paul talks about putting off and putting on certain mindsets. So let's practice.

• First, get two blank index cards.

• Next, think of the person or situation in your life that currently brings you the most anxiety.

• Ask God to make you aware of your thoughts about that person or situation.

• Then take the next 5-10 minutes and write all the thoughts He brings to mind on your first index card. *I know that this can get ugly and painful and raw, but this exercise reveals our heart meditations.*

• At the top of the second card write, "Tell me true things…"

• One-by-one, write down a truth or prayer to counteract each thought you wrote on the first card.

• Now, destroy the first card, but keep that second card in arm's reach. When those anxious, negative, dishonorable thoughts tempt you, speak the true things out loud. Through Christ's empowering, choose to think on true things.

4

Do you think I'm pretty?

The best part of beauty is that which no picture can express.

Sir Francis Bacon

English philosopher, statesman and author, (1561-1626)

I brought my share of insecurities into our marriage. Insecurities that began years before I said "I do." Growing up, I was the late-bloomer with off-brand clothes. I wore big, pale-pink glasses for most of my childhood. Freckles covered my body. And the 1980s perm became my trademark. I remember certain boys teasing me about my crunchy hair or my "upside-down" glasses. And though I tried to laugh it off on the outside, I began wrestling with insecurities over beauty and worth as I walked those elementary school hallways.

I longed to be called "beautiful" by someone other than my mother. Because something in me believed that if the world declared me "beautiful" then that meant that I was valuable. When the affirmation didn't come from peers, I questioned my worth. When I couldn't hear any accolades, I believed I needed to change in order to live up to the world's definition of amazing. By junior high, the comparison game consumed me. As if on a mental roller-coaster, I continually compared myself to the tanner, fuller-figured, more athletic, socially comfortable girls, which left me feeling as if I could never measure up.

Granted, I heard the words of Sunday School teachers insisting that God made me beautifully unique. They tirelessly taught that no one else could be the *me* He designed. I wanted to believe that my freckles and small frame were a mark of His love. But my eyes would scan the room and find the *her* I wished I could be—the *her* that received the praise—until the *me* that He designed got lost in the vanity.

Sadly, that comparison pit followed me into womanhood. Even though God opened my eyes to life in Him after my rebellious college years, I still struggled to accept the identity He declared over me. I wrestled to believe that only His opinion truly mattered. I couldn't get away from that longing to please people.

I got married while nursing those insecurities. And instead of insisting on the world's favor, I started looking to my husband to fill something in me that wasn't his responsibility to fill. I looked to him for affirmation. I wanted him to convince me of my value. I tried to do all the right things in order to receive his praise and admiration. And if he didn't give it, my insecurities flared.

We lived that way for a number of years—me secretly pining for his attention, him quietly running the other way. And when God finally answered that prayer to "change me," the breaking included the crushing of an idol. In fact, until that breaking, I had lived blind to the idol I had carved—the idol of man's approval. God began to redefine beauty to my insecure soul.

In that valley of brokenness He not only revealed my heart's meditations about marriage and my husband, He showed me that I still compared myself to others in efforts to gain approval.

We do that even as grown women—compare ourselves while seeking approval. Granted, we no longer compare sticker books or jelly shoes. *Or maybe I'm the only one who compared such trivial things.* Instead, we're tempted to compare our mothering skills or the cleanliness of our homes or our post-baby muscle tone *or lack thereof.*

We look at one another trying to figure out if we're good enough. If we make the cut. *If we're beautiful.* And when it seems we don't measure up to the world's standard, we whine or eat or get depressed. Not only that, we clamor. We hold our breath, scanning the world for someone to out-do. Because if we could just do better or look better than someone else, then we think we'd feel a sense of worth, even if only for a moment.

Sadly, that same deceptive thinking infiltrates the church.

We in the church often stare at the gifts of others in jealousy. We see how God brilliantly teaches through Suzy or serves through Sandy and we feel lesser-than. Like He skipped us over when He handed out talents *and good hair.* We evaluate our worth by holding ourselves up next to the sister we're called to love and esteem. We look to others to define our value rather than trusting the intimate, specific plans and purposes our God has for us. Until we find ourselves consumed with comparing. The enemy's lies about beauty and worth steal the joy and peace rightfully ours in Christ.

The enemy continually tries to tempt me to compare my gifts with those of others. I may read a really great book or blog post, or hear an amazing message, and inevitably my mind starts questioning. *Am I that good? Am I that pretty? Do I have what it takes? Am I of value?* Every time I entertain those kinds of thoughts, in essence I look at my God and say, "You must have made a mistake when You made me. If You really loved me, You would have designed me to be more like her." Oh how it must grieve Him when we believe such twisted thoughts.

Our gracious Father says, "Stop. Stop looking at everyone else for validation. Stop trying to measure up to some external standard of worth. Look at Me, my precious daughter. I called you by name. I designed you with purpose. I have good works set aside for you to accomplish. *Only you.* Set your gaze on Me and walk confident in the *you* that I created." *Take a moment to slowly breathe in those truths.*

When we walked through our own marital valley my God stripped everything away. For years I had yearned for others to define my identity. I idolized my man's affection and needed to know that he considered me valuable. But God faithfully took it all away. And He did so for my good. He designed us to find our worth in Him alone rather than in the opinions of other fallen humans. He desires that we define beauty as He defines beauty. Because the beauty that makes Him smile, the beauty that fulfills our longing, is the beauty hidden deep within our souls.

True Beauty

Our culture often focuses on the external to the neglect of the internal. We want everything to look good on the outside even if it's crumbling on the inside. We pour time and money into our outward beauty and give the leftovers—if any—to the attention of the soul.

But God defines beauty differently. He tells of a beauty that nothing in this physical world can distort or steal, "the hidden person of the heart, with the incorruptible beauty of a gentle and quiet spirit which is very precious in the sight of God."[1]

We can't purchase, manipulate or glue on true beauty. True beauty—that which is precious to our Maker and which satisfies our soul—spills from the heart. It comes from within. In that passage above Peter tells us of a beauty that cannot fade. Time can't wrinkle or sag the beauty that God defines. Disease can't corrupt it and death can't steal it. It's the beauty of a gentle and quiet spirit.

To be honest, I have a kneejerk reaction to the implications of "gentle" and "quiet." I mean, it's the twenty-first century. We're strong, independent women. But "gentle" in this text doesn't mean "doormat." Gentle means "meek and mild."[2] It describes one who doesn't force herself upon others. She doesn't have to prove her beauty or defend her rights. She moves slowly and purposefully, responding rather than reacting. The reason? *She trusts the movement of her God.*

---

1   1 Peter 3:3-4, NKJV.

2   Strong, "Meek" (p. 209, G4239).

57

This woman rests confident in the character of her Lord. She trusts Him to be faithful. She believes Him to fulfill His promises. And she stands secure in the declarations He makes over her. She is beauty to our God. He rewards with peace: "The meek shall inherit the land and delight themselves in abundant peace."[3] And beauty shines all over her face.

To be quiet means we have "tranquility rising from within."[4] There's a stillness in our souls. Quietness of soul comes as we trust in the sovereignty of our God. It doesn't mean that anxiety won't knock. We're human. We live in a fallen world. Anxiety over the unknown will come. But this quiet woman knows what to do with those fearful thoughts. She takes them to Him. And His promised peace guards her heart and mind.[5] True beauty arises from a quiet spirit that finds rest in the character and promises of God.

He defines true beauty. *He* gives true worth. And the beauty He offers outshines the beauty sold by our fallen world.

I had misunderstood for so long. I had placed priority on the outward, seeking to find my identity in the external. I wasted years comparing myself to others, in turn wishing *me* away. In that wishing away, I never experienced His peace. Instead, my soul lived a troubled existence. I sought to please men rather than please my God.[6] And in the pleasing, I lost the *me* He created.

Yet He has so much more for His children.

---

3   Psalm 37:11.

4   Strong, "Quiet" (p.112, G2272).

5   Philippians 4:6-7.

6   Galatians 1:10.

The Reshaping

When we as God's children choose to believe what He says about us, we walk confidently. We enter a room sure of who we are, because we're His—daughters and sons of the Most High, unique, creative, purposed and valuable. His declarations over us provide a secure foundation. The world will still tempt with its lies. The enemy will whisper despair. But God's voice speaks true things. That's why we need an arsenal of His truths continually stirring in our minds.

When the world tells me that I'm unimportant, He says, "I made you, Lara, fearfully and wonderfully."[7] When the enemy tries to convince me that I'm forgettable, He says, "My thoughts towards you, my child, are innumerable. You are always on my mind."[8] When others laugh at my meager successes, He says, "I have good things set aside for you to do. Only you."[9] When I question my identity, He whispers, "I am King and you, my daughter, are a princess."[10]

In time, I slowly started to believe what He declared. And as I chose to believe Him, at times in spite of my feelings, my confidence blossomed. I found myself walking taller rather than looking at the ground. I started to trust that I had important things to say rather than thinking that my opinion didn't matter. All because I knew what my Maker said about me.

Along with the arsenal of truths stirring in my mind, God challenged me to guard my eyes. I realized that the comparison

---

7   Psalm 139:14.

8   Psalm 139:17.

9   Jeremiah 29:11; Ephesians 2:10.

10   Jeremiah 10:10; Galatians 4:6.

and false defining of beauty began with a lingering look at some*one* or some*thing*. The look then progressed to a thought and finally formed into false belief about myself.

I began praying that I would consciously know when I was looking and comparing myself to others. And I realized that I did it continually. I continually held myself up next to all the more "beautiful" women around me. So, I started taking those comparison thoughts captive, replacing them with His words.[11] And eventually, through obedience with my mind and the empowering of His Spirit, my soul believed Him.

He made you. He formed you with purpose and plans. He crafted your eyes and sculpted your hands. He designed you to reflect Him, to know Him, to be consumed with Him—to glorify Him. And when we do, we are beauty.

The Most Beautiful Woman I Know

The Lord recently brought the most beautiful woman into my life. You'll never see her on a magazine cover. She doesn't wear fancy clothes or flashy jewelry. But she invites me and my kids over for tea parties. She sets the table with porcelain tea sets and allows my young, rambunctious boys to pour their own juice into the breakable cups. "They're fine," she insists as I nervously try to keep them from chipping the antique set.

We drink our drinks and eat lots of sweet things. Then the kids leave the table to pilfer through her toy basket, while I sit

---

11   See Chapter Three.

and glean from her every word. She's eighty-three and still reads deep books by Oswald and Lewis and Piper. Always learning. Always looking at Him.

Over the years she has walked through the death of her husband and two children. *Walked. Not collapsed under the weight of despair.* She trusts her Maker. She says that He would never allow anything to touch her that wasn't ultimately for her good and His deserved glory. She pours His love on to those graced to know her with prayers and hugs and wisdom words. Her beauty radiates, unhindered and bright. The incorruptible beauty of a gentle and quiet spirit which greatly pleases her Lord.

True beauty—the kind that doesn't fade or wrinkle—comes from within. When life crumbled, I imperfectly chose to give Him my heart. And He changed me. He whispered of my beauty, and I dared to believe Him.

SMALL GROUP DISCUSSION

- How have you struggled with equating worth to external beauty or accomplishments?

- How have you wrestled with comparison?

- What truths regarding your value can you choose to think upon when insecurities strike at your soul?

DIGGING DEEPER

The desire to please others drives us into that comparison pit. We crave man's approval in efforts to "feel" worthy. Yet true worth is found in pleasing Him.

Read the following passages, noting after each text what pleases God.

- 1 Samuel 16:7
- Romans 2:28-29
- Ephesians 6:5-6
- 1 Thessalonians 2:4
- Hebrews 11:6

When our hearts find rest and security in Him, we are beauty. As we trust what He declares about us, we walk with confidence. The world will continue to bombard us. Images of the cultural ideal for a woman won't stop just because we decide we want to walk by faith in Him. That's why we need to continually meditate on His thoughts towards us as His daughters.

Read Psalm 139. We desire to be known. God designed us that way. What are some things God says He knows about us?

It amazes me to think that God knows me so perfectly. But He doesn't just know me. In fact, I want more than His knowledge of me. We find lasting security when we grasp that He knows us completely and still loves us regardless. *Even when we're a complete mess.* What from the text points to the fact that He not only knows us, but He knows with a tender love?

How does this Psalm relate to true beauty?

We are all a work in progress. As long as we walk this earth He will continue to mold us and make us more like His Son, the most beautiful One. And though we are in process—gems in the rough—He gives glimpses of the ways He designed us beautifully unique.

List some specific ways that He created *you* individually unique.

Write a prayer of thanks for the ways He uniquely created and gifted you.

5

But I have a right to be loved

The secret of contentment is the realization that life is a gift, not a right.

Author Unknown

I never blatantly voiced it, but I believed it. They had brainwashed me. Each and every cartoon princess in her sequined gown with perfect hair brainwashed me into thinking I had certain "rights" to a man's love. I had a right to the knight in shining armor coming to my rescue. I had a right to him cherishing and pursuing me. I deserved it. I was entitled because I too was a princess. *Insert tiara here.*

I progressed through life with the princess mentality lingering in the backdrop, until I eventually met my man. Once we got engaged, good-intentioned people gave me good-intentioned books on how to have a good Christian marriage. I read about communicating my needs and my call to be his helpmate. But the phrase that meshed so nicely with the rights I had learned as a child came from Scripture: "Husbands love your wives, as

Christ loved the church and gave himself up for her."[1] Perfect. That was just what I wanted, to be loved with self-abandonment.

I would read the words written to my man about how his love could best reflect our Lord, and then I would measure him next to my "good-Christian-husband list." If on any point *he* struggled, then *I* struggled. I grew silently bitter and discontented. Then I would inwardly pout, completely missing the log that was hanging out of my own eye. *Completely missing grace.*

At times I would try to *help* him live up to the list. God defined how this marital love should look—the man loving his wife with self-abandonment. I just wanted to help enforce it. Because deep down, I believed that if my husband would do right and be right then everything else would fall into place.

But I had it all twisted. True, as His child, God loves me. I am of great value to Him. He calls me "daughter" and therefore a "princess." Being loved like Christ loves the church honors and reflects Him. He desires my husband to cherish and love me with abandonment. Those are all true things. Those things honor God. The problem, however, existed in my heart.

I clung to this beautiful love as something that would ultimately fulfill me. When my husband didn't live up to the list, I wrestled with feelings of rejection and frustration. Then, instead of being a wife who poured out grace and interceded for my husband, I selfishly demanded my biblical rights to love.

I claimed my rights because *I* wanted to be loved. *I* wanted the fairytale. I desired for my husband's love to fill *me*. Sure,

---

1   Ephesians 5:25.

I wanted my Lord reflected in our marriage. I honestly did. But I wanted Him reflected by how my man loved me. I was *entitled* to sacrificial love. Or so I thought. Meanwhile, the Lord's instructions to me as the wife sat on the back burner.

> Wives, submit to your own husbands, as to the Lord. For the husband is the head of the wife even as Christ is the head of the church, his body, and is himself its Savior. Now as the church submits to Christ, so also wives should submit in everything to their husbands.[2]

According to God's design, my husband had a "right" to my respect. He tells us as wives to submit to our husbands as we would to the Lord...in everything. To submit means that we willingly yield and cooperate.[3] It's a command. We're to do it today, presently, in whatever situations arise. But our submission goes deeper than our words or our hands. Ultimately, God looks at the heart.

God instructs us to have a heart attitude that willingly comes up under the headship of our husband as we would to the Lord. This attitude reflects Him. *Him.* This marriage idea is ultimately about Him. Not me. It's not about my rights. It's not about my husband's rights. It's about this crazy big God of ours who reigns on high and deserves continual praise and honor.

Submitting to our husbands brings glory to our Father. And He's worthy of that glory. He designed marriage to be a word picture of the gospel. That's why the enemy hates it. When we

---

2   Ephesians 5:22-24.

3   Strong, "Submit" (p. 260, G5293).

submit to our husbands, in turn submitting to our Lord, we reflect God. And there's no greater calling on our souls—no greater fulfillment.

Looking back over the first five years of our marriage, I rarely submitted from the heart. Something in me thought that my husband didn't deserve my submission if he wasn't holding up his end of the deal. If he didn't actively love me like Christ loved the church, then I wasn't going to submit. But those stipulations aren't found in the text.

I would often "submit" while disrespectful thoughts consumed my mind. And when I did outwardly yield, it was often with the underlying hope that my yielding might cause him to love me like Christ loved the church. *That's called manipulation*.

My eyes weren't focused upon God when it came to my marriage. My eyes were fixed on *me* and what my husband could do for *me*. And with that selfish vision, I convinced myself that I had a right to his selfless love.

But that mindset wore me down. By God's grace I finally stopped pointing at my man. I finally stopped insisting that he change and asked God to change me. I didn't want to depend upon my man to fill me. I wanted fullness of life found in God as described through His Word, regardless of my husband's love *or* unlove. I wanted freedom from that "rights-claiming" mentality.

The Example of our Lord

"Rights-claiming" doesn't reflect Him. In fact, Jesus exemplified something completely contradictory to my twisted way of thinking. Jesus—the God-man—actually laid down all of His rights.

Throughout eternity, He had enjoyed perfect communion with the Father.[4] His glory shone in the heavenlies.[5] He had rights to continual praise. And He received that praise continually. By Him, everything was created that was created. He was and continues to be forever Divine.

Yet, for a brief thirty-three years, this Jesus set aside His rights. He bent down and came into this fallen world. He clothed Himself with human skin and bones. He veiled the glory due His name. And "He made Himself of no reputation."[6] *No reputation.* To be really honest, I strive to maintain my reputation. In my flesh, I want the admiration and the accolades. Yet Jesus made Himself of *no* reputation.

As if that weren't enough degradation, He then humbled Himself to die a humiliating, gruesome death. Not only was the death physically excruciating, His death was the payment to a holy God for all the sins of all mankind forever. He took upon Himself the wrath that we as sinful humans deserve. The wrath that we as humans have a "right" to experience.

As He bowed before the Father with the weight of God's holy wrath on His shoulders, drops of blood appeared on Jesus' brow.[7] He laid down all of His rights to any glory, making Himself of no reputation, and then He died for me, even when I was still His enemy.[8]

---

4   John 1:1-5, 18.

5   John 1:14; Revelation 4–5.

6   Philippians 2:7-8.

7   Luke 22:44.

8   Romans 5:6-11.

He came to this earth to serve, not to be served.[9] The King of kings was born in a stable.[10] When reviled, He didn't revile in return.[11] He took out a towel and willingly washed the dirty feet of His betrayer.[12] He humbled Himself all the way down to the cursed death on a tree. And He's my example.

I'm called to follow in His footsteps. If I truly want to experience the life He described as "abundant," then the command is clear: "Jesus said to His disciples, 'If anyone would come after me, let him deny himself and take up his cross and follow me. For whoever would save his life will lose it, but whoever loses his life for my sake will find it.'"[13]

Jesus' words fly in the face of everything I'd grown to believe. In fact, as an American I grew up claiming my rights to life, liberty and the pursuit of happiness.[14] Anything less meant that I should rise up and defend what I'd been given.

But Jesus' three-part instruction to His disciples sobers the selfish heart—deny yourself, take up your cross, and follow Him. I'm pretty sure He meant for us to take it seriously, especially in regard to our marriages. But for so long I hadn't. I hadn't denied self. I hadn't "lost sight of my own interests."[15] Instead, I had elevated self. I had defended my right to be loved sacrificially. I had kept my eyes set on *me* and *my* wants. Yet, to be His

---

9   Matthew 20:28.

10   Luke 2:7.

11   1 Peter 2:23.

12   John 13:11-13.

13   Matthew 16:24-25.

14   Declaration of Independence, July 4, 1776.

15   Strong, "Deny" (p. 32, G533).

follower meant that I had to deny myself, just as He denied the glory due His name.

The call was clear. He called me to esteem my husband higher than myself. He challenged me to serve him from a heart of love rather than insist he serve me. I needed my gaze set upon my Lord rather than on my man. Self-denial needed to characterize my daily choices, or I wouldn't reflect Him.

Then He says to take up my cross, namely suffer. *Suffer?* For years I had pleaded with God to change our marriage. I didn't want to suffer. I wanted the husband who loved me like Christ loves His church. I wanted the happily-ever-after. I wanted the fairytale.

But more than my fleeting happiness, God's agenda in my life includes Him making me holy. *I may need to repeat that.* God's agenda in my life includes Him making me holy. And my transformation into a holy vessel often comes *through* suffering, by which He sheds needful things from me.

"Count it all joy, my brothers, when you meet trials of various kinds, for you know that the testing of your faith produces steadfastness. And let steadfastness have its full effect, that you may be perfect and complete, lacking in nothing."[16] Joy comes in knowing that our God faithfully works through each and every trial, refining our faith. He never leaves His children. He always moves purposefully. We can trust that if He allows a form of suffering into the lives of His children, then He does so for our good and His glory. He does so for our own transformation.

---

16   James 1:2-4.

That doesn't mean we will always understand the complete "why" of His allowances. But when we begin with His character and His promises, we can trust that ultimately His love motivates His movement in the lives of His children. *A tough thing to believe when we're in the midst of heartbreak.*

I hadn't fully trusted that the trials in my marriage could be part of His plan for my own sanctification. It seemed absurd. *Snow White never told me.* But God Almighty said it. And to be counted as His disciple, I had to take up my cross and follow. He set the example. He took the lead, denying His rightful glory and then carrying His cross to that holy mountain. And He challenged me to follow in His footsteps.

My whole world flipped upside down at the thought of my Lord. If I truly allowed His example to affect how I thought and how I lived, then it meant a complete death to my old ways. It meant a complete sacrifice of rights. In a home that appeared to be hanging by a thread, it meant a crucifixion of self. To truly follow Him with my whole heart, even as a wife in a complicated situation, He called me to deny my "rights."

Right to Leave

The journey to self-denial became more pronounced when I grappled with my "right" to walk away from our marriage. And people were quick to remind me of my right. They referred to Jesus' "exception" to divorce, encouraging me to turn the page on this marriage.[17] "He'll do it again," they insisted.

---

17   I talk about divorce at length in Chapter Six.

But I wanted clear direction from my God. The stakes were too high for anything less. So I got honest with Him, desperate for His leading. And through that communing, I knew that He wasn't releasing me. I knew it. I didn't like it, but deep down I knew it.

Throughout the early months of our healing, I consciously laid down the right to leave over and over again. Feelings can be convincing. But I actively remembered the example of my Lord. I surrounded myself with friends who spoke truth into my spirit. I crucified those rights that I had fed since childhood. And I chose to trust the call of self-denial, setting my eyes firm on Him, believing that His blessing would follow my obedience.

At times this crucifying of self brought excruciating soul-pain, but He faithfully blessed my desire to follow Him. He faithfully continued to transform me as I chose to lay down my "rights."

But I Do Have Some Rights

Even though Jesus laid down His rights and instructed us to follow His lead, in Him we do have certain rights. And this world can't steal them.

In Him, I have a right to peace, even when life appears chaotic. *Even when it looks like a tornado whipped through my heart.* He says so in the book of Philippians. He tells me not to be anxious about anything—not to preoccupy myself with worry or fear. Rather, He says to bring every anxious thought to Him in prayer, with thanksgiving. When we do, He promises that peace will guard our hearts and minds.[18] He promises. It's our right in Christ. We have a right to peace.

In Him, I have a right to be called a daughter of the King. He says that once I accept Christ's sacrifice as the covering for my sin, I can call Him "Daddy."[19] I have a royal heritage. And nothing in this world can steal my identity. I will always be His. Even if everyone else on the planet were to betray me or leave me, I have a right to be called His daughter.

In Him, I have a right to joy, even when challenges mark my journey. This doesn't mean that I have to fake happiness when the trials come. That would be ridiculous. But as James tells us, joy arises from a vibrant faith.[20] When we dare to take the Lord at His Word, believing Him to be over and around and faithful through the suffering, joy can rise up from ashes. *Joy can rise up*.

In Him, I have a right to forgiveness, even if I fail Him again and again. Jesus died for this. He laid down His life so that I could experience God's complete forgiveness for every sin I've ever committed and every sin I will ever commit. That doesn't mean I should rebel, but it does reveal my right to His grace when I'm under His salvation.[21] When I fail to die to my selfish ways, He still loves me. He still pursues my heart. He stills finishes the work He started in me.[22] I have a right to His forgiveness.

---

18 Philippians 4:6-7.

19 Galatians 4:6.

20 James 1:2-4.

21 Romans 6:1-2.

22 Philippians 1:6.

In Christ we have a rightful inheritance. He may call us to die to self and lay down our fleshly pursuits, but it's only because His blessings so far outweigh our self-agenda. He may challenge us to believe His plans for our holiness rather than demand instantaneous happiness. He may even call us to wash our betrayer's feet. But our rights in Christ cannot compare to the temporal, earthly rights we quickly want to claim. We have a right to take Him at His Word. We have a right to walk this road by faith.

SMALL GROUP DISCUSSION

• What rights have you come to believe/claim in your own heart and mind?

• What does it do to your soul when you "claim" those rights and demand your own way?

• How does Jesus' example challenge your own rights-claiming mentality?

DIGGING DEEPER

We can deceive ourselves into thinking that God chooses sides. We argue with a loved one and determine in our mind that God is right behind us, pointing out the other's faults and frustrated with their poor reflection of Him. But God doesn't choose sides. He's only on one "side"—love's side.

He *is* love. He defines love. He embodied love when He sent His Son to this earth to die. Following His humble, sacrificial example brings the greatest blessing to our souls.

Read Philippians 2:3-11. What does it look like to esteem others as better than ourselves?

Who is God challenging you to esteem as better than yourself?

Practically speaking, how does that esteeming look in the day-to-day?

Jesus remains our example. When we choose to follow after Him, setting our eyes on Him, we experience the freedom He intended for us.

Read James 3:16-18. How have you seen your own "self-seeking" stir up contention and strife in relationships?

How can you promote peace in your difficult relationships? How does laying down your personal "rights" promote peace?

Read Matthew 5:9. What are peacemakers called?

We reflect Him when we lay down our rights. We honor Him when we esteem others higher than ourselves. We mirror Him when we promote peace.

6

Leaving would mean I miss a blessing

I have known many happy marriages, but never a compatible one.
The whole aim of marriage is to fight through and survive the instant
when incompatibility becomes unquestionable.

G. K. Chesterton
English writer, (1874-1936)

Though I entered into marriage with "death do us part" mentality, as the early years of our marriage grew more challenging, divorce seemed like a great option. Focusing on my man's shortcomings (while disregarding my own) helped me avoid God's voice on the matter. The way I saw it, divorce meant I could start afresh with a more perfect man who would "love me like Jesus." And to be honest, that sounded really good.

Once our marriage reached the lowest of pits, running away seemed much more pleasant than staying in the middle of the pain. In fact, I grew up handling life's tragedies by emotionally and spiritually running away. So when people suggested divorce as the viable option, emphasizing my "right to leave," it fueled the desire to flee.

But God had different plans.

Somehow, in spite of my feelings, I became desperate for my Lord's voice. I had learned over the years that God always knows best, even if His plans mean the narrow path. So, in the middle of the pain, I determined not to let opinion drive me. I didn't want my volatile emotions to lead me. I wanted His voice to be my guide—nothing more, nothing less. That's when He spoke the word of restoration from the pages of Joel.

But I wrestled. Restoration seemed impossible. I wondered how any good could come from this cavernous breach in our marriage. Yet in spite of my questions, I sensed God saying to my spirit, "Daughter, you can go. You can walk away. I will always be with you. I will continue to transform you. But if you choose to walk away, you will miss the ultimate blessing that I have for you and your marriage. You will miss it."

I didn't want to miss it. I wanted all of Him that a human could experience—all of His blessings and all of His fullness. So if His ultimate blessing meant I needed to stay committed to this marriage, regardless of the bitter ache, then I wanted to stay committed.

But I also wanted to know why. Why would I miss a blessing if I chose to walk away? I searched His Word for answers. And what He revealed both humbled and empowered me.

Disclaimer

Before I go any deeper, I need to give a disclaimer. I am ever-aware of the statistics. I know many precious Christians who have divorce in their past or separation in their present—dear friends whom I walk beside in my own daily life. So, I pray I express myself clearly, with great humility and the love of our Lord.

If you are divorced, you have *not* committed the unpardonable sin. You will not hear condemnation from these pages. The Lord

Jesus died on a cross to take away all condemnation.[1] He is bigger than anything we may choose to do. He is bigger than anything placed upon us. He offers healing and redemption, regardless. Stand there. Believe Him for those promises.

We can't put God in some cookie-cutter box. Every situation uniquely unfolds. Every heart has crevices that only our Maker can perfectly see and know. But regardless of our individual situations, He is forever trustworthy. And His Word always reveals His will and ways.

I have one desire with this chapter. *Only one.* I long to unfold truth. I don't want opinion or speculation. I've heard enough of that from a world that craves more answers. I'm not here to judge or to avenge. I simply want to hear Him. I want God's raw, honest truth because His truth sets us free.[2] I want to know why divorce leaves deep scars.

For those who haven't walked through divorce, or even those who have never been married, it's still vital that we as the church understand God's heart. Because nearly half of all marriages end with lawyers and legalities. So with all of that in mind we progress on a journey to hear what our God says about divorce.

What Exactly Did He Say?

God doesn't warn us of things because He hates us. He doesn't allow His children to commit to challenging marriages simply to make us miserable. Love motivates our Father's movement in our

---

1   Romans 8:1.

2   John 8:32.

lives. He has infinite reason for each and every thing He instructs us to do, or *not* to do. He has infinite reason for every allowance in our lives as His sons and daughters.

When my own marriage reached the lowest point, I embraced divorce more readily because I didn't fully grasp God's design. I didn't rightly define "covenant" or fully understand my role in marriage. I was too consumed with me—my needs and my wants. But it's not about me. *It's not about you.* It's about this eternal, worthy God.

God designed marriage to reflect Himself. He means for it to be a tangible picture of Christ and the church—a tangible image of His love.[3] In this love, He poured out His life to redeem His bride from her own sin. He woos her and pursues her, graciously and tenderly. And she responds, humbly washing the feet of the One drawing her soul. He means for marriage to picture Jesus and His bride. He designed it to be evangelistic.

But we're sinful, selfish humans. We don't think about whether or not *we* look like Jesus. We focus upon whether our *spouse* looks like Jesus. And if he doesn't, then we want a new one. We want love to be easier. We want our husbands to obey and give their lives for us. *Would you die for me already?!* But our Lord is more interested in transforming us into a holy love vessel than in bringing about our fleeting happiness.[4] He uses the context of marriage to sanctify us so that we would more clearly reflect Him. Thankfully, He doesn't cast us aside when we fall or

---

3   Ephesians 5:23-32.

4   Thomas, Gary, *Sacred Marriage*, Grand Rapids, Zondervan: 2000.

fail. He patiently prods us and slowly transforms us into a more glorious image. And He does so out of His immeasurable grace.

Ultimately, divorce misrepresents our Lord. Divorce takes what He created—this image of Christ and His bride—and handles it treacherously. Back in the book of Malachi, the priests were handling marriage treacherously:

"Judah has dealt treacherously, and an abomination has been committed in Israel and in Jerusalem, for Judah has profaned the LORD's holy institution which He loves: He has married the daughter of a foreign god."[5]

First, they disregarded His instructions and took foreign wives who worshiped pagan gods. They intermarried. And God says that in doing so they committed an abomination. They profaned what He created. They mishandled His design for marriage by becoming one with a pagan people. Out of His love and eternal vision, He commands His children—believers—to marry believers. He doesn't say that to punish us or harm us or keep us from something better. He always guides out of love. Any stipulations He gives, He gives for our good and His glory.

Out of His great love, God gives the command to marry a fellow believer to protect us. He knows that the oneness in marriage runs deep. And He desires we become one with a spouse who loves and honors Him.

When we marry, we are no longer two. God makes us one flesh with the other person. *Maybe that's why we start to look alike.* He doesn't just put us side-by-side. He doesn't just clump

---

5   Malachi 2:11, NKJV.

us under one roof. He literally makes us one, fusing us together as one flesh.[6] I'm not sure we could ever fully grasp what takes place on a spiritual and emotional level when we say "I do" before a holy God. But I know this: in His eyes, we are one.[7]

When we covenant together with our spouse before this holy God, *He* makes us one. We become one with our spouse's strengths and one with their weaknesses. We become one with their worldview and one with their body. That's why Jesus said, "What therefore God has joined together, let not man separate."[8]

Back in the book of Malachi the priests took foreign wives, so God declared they be "cut off from the tents of Jacob."[9] They defiled God's design, therefore consequences had to follow. He loved them and wanted His blessing to rest upon them. But His blessing could not rest upon their disobedience.

I know that some may be thinking, "But Lara, I *did* marry an unbeliever. Now what?" Paul actually addresses this in his letter to the church at Corinth:

> If any woman has a husband who is an unbeliever, and he consents to live with her, she should not divorce him. For the unbelieving husband is made holy because of his wife, and the unbelieving wife is made holy because of her husband. Otherwise your children would be unclean, but as it is, they are holy. But if the unbelieving partner separates, let it be so. In such cases the brother or sister is not enslaved. God has called you to peace. For how do you know, wife, whether you will

---

6   Malachi 2:15.

7   Malachi 2:15.

8   Matthew 19:6.

9   Malachi 2:12.

save your husband? Or how do you know, husband, whether you will save your wife?[10]

Maybe you married an unbeliever. But as my mama always reminds me, "Bloom where you are planted." God is bigger! He is grace. If you married an unbeliever and he (or she) is willing to stay married to you as the believing spouse, then bloom there. Reflect Jesus all the more, in all His grace and mercy and love. Who knows if you will save your spouse?

I know—*I know*—this is easier said than done. It just is. Our hearts feel things and want things. And when we don't receive the love from our spouse that we so desperately crave, it absolutely hurts. But the kind of love God calls us to stretches beyond feeling. His love is an act of the will; emotions eventually follow. He blesses the choice to love regardless.

Back in the Malachi text, intermarrying wasn't all they did to dishonor God's design. They also dealt treacherously with the wife of their youth—"[their] companion and...wife by covenant."[11] They divorced their wives, disregarding the covenant they had made. And it grieved God.[12] He explained that divorce "covers [one's] garment with violence."[13] *Stay with me.*

In the marriage covenant, God serves as our covering. The text says He gives us a remnant of His Spirit.[14] In some respect, He Himself is our outer garment. Jewish men and women express this

---

10   1 Corinthians 7:13-16.

11   Malachi 2:14.

12   Malachi 2:16.

13   Malachi 2:16.

14   Malachi 2:15.

"covering" through their use of a prayer shawl. They ceremonially drape these over their heads and then over their shoulders for prayer, signifying the enveloping of the Lord over them.

During the Jewish wedding ceremony they use the prayer shawl to cover the husband and wife together, also signifying the covering of the Lord God Himself over their union. *He* covers and makes them one. Just as He covers and makes us one with our spouse.

When we divorce, it's as if we hide violence with His holy covering. We take what He made to be one and try to rip it apart. We rip apart one flesh. *No wonder it is so painful.* Divorce misrepresents His wooing love towards His own bride—a love undeserved, relentless, and priceless. That's why He tells us to "take heed," be on guard, so we do not deal treacherously with His holy design.[15]

For years, I had no idea of the depth of oneness. I thought a piece of paper from the local courthouse could abolish what God had fused together. I thought I could seamlessly start afresh with someone "better." I had grown complacent towards my man and towards this thing called "marriage." I had dealt treacherously with His design. Yet He gave grace. He convicted and cleansed and redeemed the broken places.

Of Greater Concern

Even if physical divorce doesn't mark our experience, we need to be on guard. I look back over the first six years of my marriage and know that I handled marriage poorly. I was physically present

---

15   Malachi 2:16.

in my home, but my heart lived far from my husband. I inwardly dealt treacherously with this man to whom I had vowed my love. I tore him down in my mind and criticized his weaknesses. I craved for him to meet my own love-needs instead of allowing my God to fill me that I might meet his needs. And over time, my heart grew hard.

When Jesus stepped foot on this fallen earth, He pierced hearts. He showed us that the external is useless if the internal is corrupt. When it comes to marriage, "sticking it out" isn't enough. To truly honor God's design, I need a tender heart towards my spouse and towards marriage. Yet so many of us live jaded and detached—sharing physical space in a physical world but with hardened hearts.

Let that not be said of us. *Let that not be said of me.*

Marriage serves as the context for transformation. In it I crucify this self-focused life. I lay down my own desires—even honorable desires—over and over and over again. But as I do, He graciously transforms me to look more like His Son. He allows me to picture this One who washed the feet of His friends, even the feet of the one who would betray and deny Him.

This day we have choice. As much as depends upon us, we can choose to reflect God's design, regardless of our spouse's choices. Even if our spouse rejects us or leaves us, we can still remain faithful. We can still point passionately to our Lord, reflecting Him to a world in dire need of salvation.

It may be the most excruciating thing you or I ever do, especially when we walk through seasons where love is not returned, but He honors the one who honors Him. He lifts those who humble themselves. He blesses obedience.

I Almost Missed It

I saw a friend at church the other day. The last I had heard, her marriage was struggling. She and her spouse were separated. So I asked, "How's everything going?" She went on to share the change that had happened in their home.

"Lara, I almost missed it," she said with tears in her eyes. "I was just so tired and over it. He was out of the house and in many ways that made things easier. It's only by God's grace that I didn't completely close off my heart. Because God has done something miraculous in our home. And I almost missed it."

In spite of feelings, and regardless of what may seem like a hopeless situation, the Lord may challenge you to stay committed in your heart, regardless of the *un*love of your spouse. He may dare you to stay because He may want to do something wildly miraculous in your home. Only He can guide you through the dark places, but one thing's for sure: we don't want to miss His "wildly miraculous."

SMALL GROUP DISCUSSION

- How do these thoughts on divorce challenge you?

- How do these thoughts on divorce encourage you?

- How do you remain soft towards your spouse? Or how can you soften your heart towards your spouse?

- Practically speaking, what choices can you personally make to reflect God's design in your own marriage, even in the season you are currently walking?

DIGGING DEEPER

It's become a mantra in my own soul: "How would love look right now, in this moment?" Because it's all about love. If I'm not exhibiting love, then I'm missing the point.

Read John 13:34-35. What does love reveal to the world?

Read Matthew 5:43-47. Who are we called to love? Why?

Our love—especially for those who we would consider our "enemies"—reveals who it is we follow. But let's be honest. Most times we don't "feel" like loving those who hurt us or persecute us. Yet I'm sure Jesus didn't "feel" like dying on the cross for those hurling insults. But He did it as an act of love following the will of the Father. And God highly exalted Him.

Love isn't easy. It's death to self. It's taking up our own cross and following Jesus' lead. It's a choice of the will. Read 1 Corinthians 13. Note every aspect of love you read in that chapter.

Which aspect of love reveals your place of greatest challenge? Why?

Read John 13:1-15. Jesus even washed the feet of His betrayer, Judas. How does the example of our Lord inspire you?

We cannot love like Jesus loves on our own. But thankfully He equips us to live selflessly and victoriously through the power of His Spirit and the sword of His Word.

Write out a prayer to the Lord. Confess any places of *un*love and ask Him to minister to your own heart—enabling you to love even those who aren't able to love you in return.

7

Choosing to remember no more

Forgiveness is the fragrance the violet sheds on the heel that has crushed it.

Mark Twain
American author, (1835-1910)

In the days following my discovery of the betrayal, revenge felt so right. My heart justified it. Every breath took effort, every tear stung, and every thought fed the anger. And though our merciful God did allow me some time to grieve, He wouldn't let me stay in that place of bitterness. For bitterness poisons the soul.[1]

Soon after entering our marital pit, I emailed a professor who had impacted me during my studies at seminary. I told him the guarded, short version of our story—secretly hoping and assuming he would take *my* side. I wanted him to say things like, "You poor thing" or "Do you want me to hurt him for you?" But instead, he pointed me to Jesus. Granted, he did it with tenderness and empathy for my pain. But he quoted my Lord. And to be honest, I got a little irritated.

---

1   Acts 8:23.

"If you do not forgive others their trespasses, neither will your Father forgive your trespasses."[2] Are you kidding me? The thought of "forgiving" made me nauseous. In my mind, Adam didn't deserve my forgiveness. So, I wrestled to find a way around the words of my God. But beneath all my emotions and justifications, I knew He was calling me to live beyond myself. I knew He was calling me to forgive. I just wasn't sure how to get past my heart. I wasn't sure what forgiveness actually looked like. So I asked God to guide me.

Foundation

He began by revealing my own desperation. Somehow over the years I had forgotten the great grace covering *me*. I had been the prodigal. I had run hard and fast away from my Lord. Yet in spite of me, God pursued. He woke me. And then He forgave my mess of a life and began a transforming work. I had forgotten the grace I was under. I acted like whiny Jonah. Remember him?

After Jonah repented from the belly of a fish for blatantly disobeying the voice of the Lord, the fish spat him on to dry land. Then he went to Nineveh, the place infamous for their evil ways. Jonah assumed that they would ignore his plea for repentance, secretly hoping to see the wrath of God fall upon them. Instead, the entire city repented, crying out to God for mercy. And God gave it. Then Jonah whined.[3] He complained. He didn't want God to pour out grace upon his enemy. He wanted revenge. He liked

---

2   Matthew 6:15.

3   Jonah 4.

having God's grace for himself. But he wanted vengeance on his enemies.

But that's not how our God works.

The Lord does unimaginable things: like when He planned redemption. He looked at His creation—rebelling and blaspheming His name—and then, out of His love, He made a way for us to be restored. He sacrificed His own perfect, holy, beautiful Son, Jesus, for the sin of His enemies. *His enemies!* He sent His own Son to drink the cup of wrath due to those who didn't honor Him. *Who does that?*

Then His Son defeated death—the consequence of sin. He took away the judgment due to me from a holy God, declaring me freed and cleansed and righteous. It's a radical plan. *He's* radical. And we're all desperate for His mercy and grace.

Regardless of how far we've run from God, all of us stand before Him completely depraved. All of us come to Him desperate for His grace. Next to His holiness, we all deserve His wrath. He is the One clothed in splendor and glory with these heavenly creatures continually declaring praise.[4] *We are not.*

After reading the email from my professor encouraging me to forgive, I needed to remember who I was, *and Who I wasn't.* I enter God's courts solely because of His grace.[5]

Tactic

Remembering His grace over *me* put me in the heart-position to forgive my man. But I needed to know *how.* I wanted to know

---

4   See Isaiah 6.

5   Hebrews 10:19-22.

what forgiveness practically looked like. So, I camped out with Jesus' words from the book of Luke: "Pay attention to yourselves! If your brother sins, rebuke him, and if he repents, forgive him, and if he sins against you seven times in the day, and turns to you seven times, saying, 'I repent,' you must forgive him."[6]

In this text Jesus spoke to "brothers," or Christ-followers.[7] He assumed that on this life journey, our brothers and sisters—those who love Jesus—*will* sin against us. They will sin against us and we will sin against them because we're all in process. We're *all* in process.

Regardless of how long we've walked with the Lord, He's still transforming us to look more and more like His Son. On this side of Christ's return, we *will* sin against one another in thought, word, and deed. In fact, we should expect it. So *when* fellow believers sin against us, Jesus says to rebuke them. To *rebuke* means to admonish or straightly charge.[8] In other words, He calls us to communicate clearly and honestly.

Let me just tell you. I am a natural born people-pleaser. I avoided conflict from an early age. So, learning to communicate about a wrong has stretched me beyond my natural self. I'd much prefer to sweep things under the proverbial rug. But God desires unity among believers.[9] He desires unity in our homes. Unity reflects Him. Divisiveness doesn't. [10] To promote unity after a wrong, He calls us to communicate after a breach.

---

6   Luke 17:3-4.

7   Strong, "Brothers" (p. 5, G80).

8   Strong, "Rebuke" (p. 100, G2008).

9   Ephesians 4:1-6.

10   Romans 16:17-18.

The cavernous gap in our own marriage definitely needed addressing. Forgiveness meant that I had to communicate. But before I could rebuke, especially with such a tender ache, I had to spend time alone with my God. I needed His perspective. I needed Him to touch my own wound and give me His vision for my man. Otherwise, I knew it wouldn't be pretty. *Even then, it wasn't very pretty.*

Whether we avoid conflict by nature or thrive on it, it's vital to gain His perspective. For some (like me), gaining His perspective empowers us to confront. For others, seeing with His vision softens the rebuke. Either way, we need to seek Him first. Whenever I desire to gain His perspective I step away from daily living and get really honest with my God. King David did it throughout the Psalms, so I figure He can handle my own raw emotion. I tell Him exactly how I feel. *Out loud.*

Once emotionally bare before Him, I start preaching to myself. I declare true things about my God: "You, Lord, are faithful and motivated by Your immeasurable love." I recite truths about His character and remind my heart and mind of His promises. I sing praise songs and read His Word aloud. And eventually, He quiets my soul. It often takes time. *We need to allow ourselves time.* It takes a diligent pressing into Him. But He promises that those who seek Him with their whole heart will find Him.

He faithfully ministered when I needed His perspective for my marriage. Through that time of seeking, He enlightened me to something I hadn't really considered. He challenged me to see my husband as my brother in Christ. *I had to let that thought settle for a while.* My husband is my brother in Christ.

In time, I embraced the idea that *my brother* needed a sister in Christ to come alongside him. My brother needed a sister in Christ to speak forgiveness words over him. But it was a radical call. Sisterly love went beyond what my human strength could even conceive of doing. But I noticed that as I looked at him through the lens of "brotherhood," my stance changed. My defenses dropped and my heart softened, because it wasn't about me anymore. It was about my God being glorified in the way that I loved.

After a number of weeks of physical separation, the time finally came for us to communicate openly and honestly. God had graciously prepared us both. And though the conversation was difficult and emotional, we both knew that the road to healing began with honest conversation.

Back to Jesus' words in the book of Luke: He says that after we rebuke our brother or sister, we are to wait and listen to their reply. If they repent, then we forgive them. "Repent" means "to change one's mind, think differently about a subject, and/or have regret for previous action."[11] If our brother or sister repents—agreeing that they have sinned against us, and desiring to turn away from that behavior—then He instructs us to forgive them. We do have choice. We could choose *not* to forgive. But He commands, "Forgive." And He commands out of love.

God knows us better than we know ourselves. He knows what entangles our souls as well as what brings us the greatest joy. He knows us perfectly. We can trust that His commands to us,

---

11   Strong, "Repent" (p. 162, G3340).

even to forgive the most painful of wrongs, flow from His love. His commands are ultimately for our good. If we choose *not* to forgive, then in essence we choose His discipline. Because He chastens those He loves.[12]

To forgive literally means "to let go."[13] When we forgive, we let go of our own personal judgment and release the one who wronged us to the righteous, perfect Judge. We release them, in turn releasing ourselves.

When the temptation arises to think about past sins committed against us we have to make the deliberate choice to remind ourselves that we forgave those offenses—bringing every thought into submission to the mind of Christ. Otherwise we will find ourselves back in the valley, consumed with bitterness. As we choose to bring our thoughts back to the place of forgiveness, emotions eventually follow. They do. Eventually.

I "rebuked." My husband repented. To remain under God's blessing, I had to choose to let it all go...regardless of how I felt.

Any Stipulations?

Life gets messy. Things rarely go by the textbook. So let's address the "sticky" aspects of forgiveness.

First, what if the one who sinned against us isn't a brother or sister in the Lord? Then what? I think the words of Christ Himself—as His enemies physically tortured Him on the cross—give us a good starting place. "Father, forgive them, for they know not

12   Proverbs 3:11-12.

13   Strong, "Forgive" (p. 48, G863).

what they do."[14] Christ uttered these words while His enemies brutally murdered Him. If anyone ever had the right to be unforgiving, then the Son of God—holy and perfect—had the right. But instead, He released their sin—He let it go—and interceded on their behalf. Likewise, if an unbeliever sins against us, then our burden should be for his or her soul: "Father forgive him, he doesn't know what he's doing."

The Bible teaches that sin enslaves those who have not accepted the sacrifice of Christ. So when unbelievers sin against us, they're doing exactly what they're "supposed" to do. They sin because sin has them bound. Giving unbelievers the cold shoulder will not point them to the One they need. The love of God, shown through forgiveness, will convict their hearts and lead them to salvation.[15]

This may be the most difficult thing we ever do. The offenses of others hurt. Words slung in anger can tear us apart.[16] Unless we've died to ourselves this day, we will take everything personally and hold continual grudges. But God has more for us. He has freedom, not bondage.

Learning to die daily will come with opposition. Our emotions will tempt us and the enemy will lie, but He equips us for victory. By His power we can reflect Him through the gift of forgiveness even to an unbeliever. Even when our hearts hurt.

The second aspect of the Luke passage that proves "sticky" arises if our brother or sister doesn't repent after a rebuke. In that case, either we misunderstood their behavior or they can't see

---

14   Luke 23:34.

15   1 Peter 3:1-2.

16   Proverbs 18:21.

their own sin. Regardless of why they don't repent, we get back on our knees. If *after* talking to God we truly believe that the person is blind to their sin, then we can follow Jesus' instruction:

> If your brother sins against you, go and tell him his fault, between you and him alone. If he listens to you, you have gained your brother. But if he does not listen, take one or two others along with you, that every charge may be established by the evidence of two or three witnesses. If he refuses to listen to them, tell it to the church. And if he refuses to listen even to the church, let him be to you as a Gentile and a tax collector.[17]

Note that He doesn't say "talk to everyone you know about that person in the name of prayer requests." *Ouch*. If our brother or sister is stuck in a pattern of sin, and he or she will not hear our humble and loving rebuke—*humble* and *loving*—then we move on to the next step. At that point, we approach them again with one or two other (mature and trusted) believers to address the sin. If he or she still doesn't hear, then Jesus instructs us to tell the matter to the church—which should be done prayerfully and in submission to our pastors and elders. If our brother or sister still refuses repentance, then He tells us to treat him or her as a heathen and tax collector. And we know how Jesus treated heathens and tax collectors.

He showed grace and love to "sinful heathens." He approached the rebellious and even called some of them to be His followers. He conversed with those rejected by society. He met people where they were—and thankfully He still does. He pierced the heart and led individuals to repentance by His great love. Ultimately, He

---

17   Matthew 18:15-17.

wanted people to see their cavernous need for a Savior. In fact, if we're really honest, you and I are the heathens and the tax collectors in our flesh. We're the ones desperate for redemption—just as those who have sinned against us.

Though Jesus interacted with and loved those worn down in sin, His closest friends were those who desired to love and obey Him. Likewise, the Word instructs us to withdraw ourselves from those who continue in sin, that we might stay pure.[18] Marriage, however, brings another aspect to the table. In marriage, we covenant together with our spouse before God. And the oneness He designed reveals that He doesn't desire that we fully withdraw. So, we turn to the wisdom of Peter: "Likewise, wives, be subject to your own husbands, so that even if some do not obey the word, they may be won without a word by the conduct of their wives, when they see your respectful and pure conduct."[19] He calls us to win others with our actions.

That brings us back to square one. Whether a person repents or not, whether they're a believer or not, He calls us to forgive. He instructs us to "let it go" and release the other to a holy God—for our sake and theirs.

What If I Don't!

We can't pay the cost of unforgiveness. Jesus explains, "For if you forgive others their trespasses, your heavenly Father will also forgive you, but if you do not forgive others their trespasses,

---

18   See Romans 16:17; 1 Corinthians 5:9; 2 Thessalonians 3:6, 14; 2 John 10.

19   1 Peter 3:1-2.

neither will your Father forgive your trespasses."[20] When we choose unforgiveness, we choose to live under the judgment of God. That means we stand condemned.

We learn from Paul that "There is therefore now no condemnation for those who are in Christ Jesus."[21] If Christ truly resides in us, then we will desire to obey His instruction to forgive. We may not *feel* like forgiving, but in our spirits we will know that forgiveness brings His greatest blessing. If, however, we often harbor a bitter, unforgiving spirit towards others, then it could be evidence that we have not actually understood and accepted Christ's sacrifice. And if that's the case, then we stand already condemned. And we need a Savior.[22]

How often…really?

I can give second chances fairly easily. Third and fourth chances come with only slight hesitation. But when it comes to fifth and sixth and seventh chances, I'm tempted to write the person off for poor handling of my heart. So how often should we *really* forgive a brother who sins against us? Peter asked the same question.

"'Lord, how often will my brother sin against me, and I forgive him? As many as seven times?' Jesus said to him, 'I do not say to you seven times, but seventy-seven times.'"[23] Jesus then gave a parable of a master who forgave a servant's enormous debt. The

---

20 Matthew 6:14-15.

21 Romans 8:1.

22 As long as we walk this earth it's never too late to repent of our sin and come under the sacrifice of Christ. If you have never accepted Him as Lord, I pray that today would be the day of your salvation.

23 Matthew 18:21-22.

servant—now under the forgiveness and mercy of his master—goes and demands a smaller debt from a fellow servant. "And in anger his master delivered him to the jailers, until he should pay all his debt. So also my heavenly Father will do to every one of you, if you do not forgive your brother from your heart."[24] God takes an unforgiving heart very seriously.

We as followers of Christ—dwelling under the great mercy of God on high—should continually be ready to forgive the offenses of others, just as God forgives us under the covering of Christ. It's a high calling – one that I can't possibly obey in my flesh. Forgiveness as He describes has to be a work of His Spirit within me.

I can almost hear the wrestling within some of you. "But you don't know what I've been through!" Oh, friend, you are certainly right. I don't. I don't know your personal hurts. I don't know how life has ripped at your soul. But our heavenly Father sees every detail of our hearts. He holds every tear we cry. And He mends broken souls. No one but our Lord can fully understand your tattered spirit. But I truly believe the Word to be truth—even when our emotions rage. I believe Jesus meant for us to forgive any and all offenses. I believe He wants to enable us to let go of every single sin against us, that we might be free from resentment and festering anger.

If someone has sinned against you—either devastatingly or in the daily grind of life—then the enemy has already won a small victory. Don't let him win the war. Let's not allow him to steal the joy Christ died to give us. Under the shed blood of our risen Lord, victory is rightfully ours. In the power of *His* might, we can choose

---

24   Matthew 18:34-35.

to remember the offenses no more. He gives us weapons mighty in Him for bringing every thought into submission to truth. He can strengthen us to stand in the pain—stand with a forgiving heart. I know because He enabled me. He is a faithful Father and sovereign Lord. We can trust Him.

How Trust Relates To Forgiveness

I've been guilty of giving my heart to people. In essence, I hand them my soul, assuming they will handle it perfectly. And in doing so, I give them the power to control me. When they fail to live up to my expectations, stepping on my heart in the process, I say with slight contempt, "Because you have hurt me over and over again, I cannot trust you with my heart. You have not earned my trust." But really, Jesus never tells us to trust *people*. He says to love and forgive people. But there's only One who we can fully trust with our heart.

When we give our heart completely to our Maker, He handles it with tender care. He does shed needful things and mold it according to His will, which may mean the Refiner's fire. But He *can* be trusted. We place our heart completely in His hands, and then freely give forgiveness out of the overflow of the forgiveness we've received.

When we live in the place where our heart rests in the hands of our Maker, we find a freedom to love through forgiveness. No longer do I feel the need to clarify my forgiveness. I don't need to explain, clearly and succinctly, numerous times, that my forgiveness doesn't mean my approval of my offender's sin. Instead, I simply release them and release the judgment to the only One who judges perfectly.

This type of forgiveness flies in the face of culture. In fact, even as I type these very words I overhear a conversation at the next booth. *No exaggeration.* One woman details the betrayal of another person to her friend. The friend says, "I would never forgive that kind of betrayal." The two of them then spend twenty minutes detailing the misery that others have imposed upon them and how they could never forgive such offenses. Their souls are completely bound in bitterness.

People will continue to sin against us. And we will continue to sin against others. But choosing forgiveness means we choose life. We choose freedom. We *can* choose it again today.

SMALL GROUP DISCUSSION

- Share a time when you chose forgiveness.

- How did forgiveness free your soul?

- Share a time when you harbored unforgiveness.

- How did it bind your soul?

- What struggles do you have with forgiveness?

DIGGING DEEPER

We pay a high price when unforgiveness consumes our soul, because unforgiveness is the fertile ground that grows bitterness. And bitterness eats us from the inside out. Read Hebrews 12:14-15 and Ephesians 4:29-32. What does bitterness do to our spirit?

What does it do to our speech?

What does it do to God's Spirit?

Paul instructs us to "put away" bitterness and unforgiveness. We have to make the deliberate choice to forgive. So let's do some honest heart assessment.

Read Matthew 6:14-15, out loud. Agree with the Lord through prayer, "Lord, unforgiveness doesn't honor You. And it doesn't bring Your blessing upon me." Then ask the Lord to reveal any unforgiveness residing in your heart: "Show me, Father, if I am harboring unforgiveness." If He reveals a person that you haven't forgiven, then I challenge you to do the following:

- Write down the specific offenses you still hold with contempt.

- Spend time in prayer and ask for God's wisdom as to the next steps to take from a biblical perspective, i.e. rebuke, forgiveness, accountability, etc.

- Then release those offenses one-by-one to the One who rightly judges.

- Finally, burn—or flush—that list and choose in the daily moments of life to remember that thing no more.

Unforgiveness hurts *us* more than it hurts those who have sinned against us. Let's put it away.

8

Waiting in belief

Faith sees the invisible, believes the unbelievable, and receives the impossible.

Corrie Ten Boom
Dutch Christian writer, speaker
and survivor of the Nazi Holocaust, (1892-1983)

God spoke a restoration promise over our home. Through His Word He said, "I will restore to you the years that the swarming locust has eaten."[1] And though everything in me wanted to believe Him, restoration didn't happen overnight. And when I couldn't see physical evidences of the promise being fulfilled, I questioned. I wondered if I had actually heard Him. I wondered if I had imagined His voice coming off those pages of Scripture. But He kept calling me back to a place of faith.

I remember one Sunday. Time had slowly passed. Adam and I had been counseled through the darkest places of our marriage. Friends had prayed us out of despair. We both wanted to move forward, yet many aspects of our relationship felt the same. We still wrestled with familiar issues. And though words of faith came out of my mouth, deep in my spirit I doubted whether full restoration

---

1 Joel 2:25.

would ever be our experience. That morning our pastor preached from the book of Luke. And I knew he was preaching directly to me.

He began by mentioning the great faith of Elizabeth and Zechariah. The Word says that they walked blameless with their God, "But..."[2] But? They walked blameless, but? In spite of their obedient walking with their God, they had struggled with infertility for years, leaving them childless. And in that day and culture that meant they wrestled against shame. They walked blameless, yet a burden of shame followed them.

Then my pastor warned us against growing comfortable in our difficulties as Zechariah had done. An angel of the Lord came and spoke directly to him: "Do not be afraid, Zechariah, for your prayer has been heard, and your wife Elizabeth will bear you a son, and you shall call his name John. And you will have joy and gladness, and many will rejoice at his birth."[3] But Zechariah had grown to *expect* more suffering. He had become complacent to God's miraculous ability to do the unimaginable. So he doubted, "How shall I know this? For I am an old man, and my wife is advanced in years. "[4]

Though Zechariah had prayed for a miracle child, he no longer believed that God would answer. Even when an angel proclaimed the good news, Zechariah doubted. He set his eyes on the physical facts rather than the abilities of God Almighty to work wondrous things. So the angel spoke discipline, "You

2   Luke 1:6-7.

3   Luke 1:13-14.

4   Luke 1:18.

will be silent and unable to speak until the day that these things take place, because you did not believe my words, which will be fulfilled in their time."[5]

I found comfort in the fact that God still fulfilled His promise of a son in spite of Zechariah's unbelief. But God did discipline Zechariah for not believing. He took away his voice for nine months. Nine months. Unable to speak. Since God allows me to speak to women's groups, that particular discipline shook me.

I sat in that familiar Sunday seat with tears in my eyes. I wanted to fall down to the ground and shout out to my God, confessing my complacent unbelief, but I figured I would get a bunch of looks. So I just sat with my heart pounding and my spirit bowing before Him. *Oh, the insecurities that still plague.* I didn't want to be like Zechariah, walking around in unbelief. I didn't want to fall under God's discipline for my hardened heart.

After that sermon I spent time in the book of Hebrews pouring over the faith of those who had gone before me. Through faith, Enoch didn't die. Noah constructed an ark. Abraham left his homeland. Sarah had a child in her old age. The people crossed the Red Sea on dry land. The walls of Jericho came down. *Just to name a few.* And then I read, "Through faith...[they] obtained promises."[6] Through faith.

They couldn't obtain His promises unless they believed. Noah had to build that ark in faith before ever seeing a drop of rain. Abraham had to pack up his family and start his trek in faith without a clue as to where God was leading. And the people had to walk around the thick, strong walls of Jericho in faith

5   Luke 1:20.

6   Hebrews 11:33.

regardless of how foolish it looked to their enemy. They couldn't obtain God's promises until they chose to actively believe Him.

Active faith puts feet to our words. Active faith causes us to *do* things in movement towards His promise before we ever experience the *fulfillment* of His promise. He calls us to an active faith. It's what pleases Him: "And without faith it is impossible to please him, for whoever would draw near to God must believe that he exists and that he rewards those who seek him."[7]

It pleases my God when I believe Him. When I trust that He will fulfill His promises and remain true to His Word, He smiles over me. When I rest in His love, believing that He has good plans, I honor Him. An active faith brings Him pleasure.

My God was calling me to radically believe Him. He was challenging me to take Him at His Word—to believe with everything in me that He would indeed work full restoration into our marriage and full restoration into my own stubborn heart. He challenged me to believe that joy and gladness would be ours even though I couldn't always see it with my physical eyes. Even though we both still battled old patterns of selfish behavior.

I imperfectly chose to stand there.

Two Types of Promises

God speaks promises. And since He cannot tell a lie, His promises *will* come to pass. They will. It's just a matter of time. In that space of time between His spoken promise and the fulfilled promise, we have choice as to what we do in our hearts and minds. And our choice affects things.

---

7   Hebrews 11:6.

We can believe that He will bring about those promises. Or we can *not* believe. We can trust that He will bring down the wall. Or we can think it's impossible. Faith brings peace. Unbelief stirs anxiety. It sounds pretty simple on paper, but admittedly it's harder when we're battling our own deceptive hearts that crave physical proof.

Life happens and we doubt. We grow impatient with God's timetable and want tangible evidence. We need proof that He still sees us and loves us. We sound like Jesus' disciples.

> As they were talking about these things, Jesus himself stood among them, and said to them, "Peace to you!" But they were startled and frightened and thought they saw a spirit. And he said to them, "Why are you troubled, and why do doubts arise in your hearts? See my hands and my feet, that it is I myself. Touch me, and see. For a spirit does not have flesh and bones as you see that I have." And when he had said this, he showed them his hands and his feet. And while they still disbelieved for joy and were marveling, he said to them, "Have you anything here to eat?" They gave him a piece of broiled fish, and he took it and ate before them. [8]

Whenever I read that passage I think, "How could they not get it?" Jesus physically stood in front of them, showing them His hands and feet, yet they still couldn't get past the fact that crucified people don't come out of graves. But I love that Jesus remained soft to their humanity. He met them in the midst of their doubts and asked them for some food. He then ate in front of them to once again "prove" that He had physically risen from the grave. And finally, they believed.

---

8   Luke 24:36-43.

We're just like them. *I'm* just like them. I want to know how, when, and why. I want to touch the proof. But faith means we rest in the faithfulness of God. It means we believe Him in spite of what our physical eyes can see. It means we trust Him to bring about His promises in His perfect timing.

He gives two types of promises in His Word: conditional and unconditional. His unconditional promises happen regardless, like when He says to His children, "I will never leave you nor forsake you."[9] These types of promises don't depend upon our feeble actions. They come to pass simply because He is.

But conditional promises have stipulations. They have "ifs" attached. "If you abide in me, and if my words abide in you, ask whatever you wish, and it will be done for you."[10] *If* I abide in Him and *if* His words abide in me, *then* the things I ask will be done. Conditions, when we do the "ifs," we obtain the promises.

God had graciously spoken a promise over our marriage, but I needed to believe Him. I had to trust that He would move in His perfect time. Believing Him brought hope and rest of soul. Believing Him meant we would obtain His promises.

The Testing of Faith

Faith comes with a cost. It grows in the valleys. It blooms most vibrant where the ground seems completely desolate. I don't know why He designed it that way, but He did. It's through the darkest seasons of life that our faith can become fierce.

---

9   Hebrews 13:5-6.

10   John 15:7.

In his letter to fellow believers, James encourages, "Count it all joy, my brothers, when you meet trials of various kinds, for you know that the testing of your faith produces steadfastness. And let steadfastness have its full effect, that you may be perfect and complete, lacking in nothing."[11]

We will "meet trials." My daddy used to say, "Either you are going through a trial, you just went through a trial, or a trial is on the horizon." This side of Christ's return, trials will come. We can just plan on it. But James says that we can move through these various types of trials with joy. *Joy?*

When my heart wounds were fresh, the last thing I *felt* was joy. To be honest, I felt bitter and angry. I wanted to defend my rights. I wanted to get revenge. But as I sought the Lord's wisdom, He began to mend those places. And He unfolded James' words.

This "counting it joy" isn't a feeling. It's a resolve. When we begin to taste the soul-victory that comes in choosing to simply believe God, joy wells up. When we believe that God will remain faithful to His promises, we tap into that abundant life Christ died to give us as His followers. When we dare to take God at His word, He gives a peace that this world cannot explain. He stirs up hope in situations where despair makes more sense.

Faith means we're convinced that God will absolutely perform what He has promised, even if we can't see physical proof today.[12] Valleys will test that faith. But when we choose to trust God through the darkest of seasons—enduring to the end—we obtain His promises.

---

11   James 1:2-4.

12   Hebrews 11:1.

When I couldn't see physical proof, I had to choose to believe. If I truly wanted to experience full restoration in our marriage, I needed to trust that my God would bring it about in His perfect timing regardless of what I saw. He blesses a steadfast faith.[13]

SMALL GROUP DISCUSSION

- Share a time in your life when your faith was greatly tested. How did God minister to you in that time?

- What are some unconditional promises found in God's Word?

- What are some conditional promises found in God's Word?

- Practically speaking, how can we remain steadfast—believing God's promises—through the trials?

DIGGING DEEPER

He wouldn't call it a "test" of faith if it was easy. Faith is learned, one day at a time. But when we dare to take God at His Word, He pours

---

13   James 1:12.

life into us. I mentioned portions of this text in this chapter, but spend some time reading through Hebrews 11:1–12:2. This text is dense with encouragement as it gives examples of those who have gone before us *by faith*. As you read, note anything that really jumps off the page and speaks to your spirit:

Now, I want to lead us through a very simple Bible study method to help us glean from this text.[14] Read the passage again, this time noting any truths you discover. It could be a truth about God's character or a truth about who we are in Christ. Simply list any truth you find in the text:

Now, read the text again noting any promises that you discover. Identify whether each promise is unconditional (U) or conditional (C). If it is conditional, then note the attached condition:

Finally, read the text a fourth time, looking for commands. List them below:

---

14   For a complete explanation of this study method, you can read the book that Katie Orr and I wrote called *Savoring Living Water*, available at www.QuenchBible.com.

What is God challenging you to believe in response to this passage? How does He want you to apply what you read?

9

Prayer that changes things

A man may study because his brain is hungry for knowledge, even Bible knowledge. But he prays because his soul is hungry for God.

Leonard Ravenhill
English Christian evangelist and author, (1907-1994)

I can't explain it, but I experience its outworking. I can't physically see what happens when my words leave my mouth, but life changes as a result. I change.

In recent years, God has said "yes" to more of my prayers. But it isn't because He likes me better or hears me more clearly. It's because my prayers have changed. My desires have changed. They now flow more in line with His will.

He Gives Whatever I Want
The Psalmist says, "Delight yourself in the LORD, and he will give you the desires of your heart."[1] It's tempting to read those words and think, "Yes! Genie in a bottle, come to mama!" Yeah. *No.* God has conditions attached to those verses. He gives us the

---

1   Psalm 37:4.

desires of our heart *after* we delight in Him. To delight in Him means we remain pliable in His hands.[2] It means we trust Him and "befriend faithfulness."[3]

As we delight in Him, He transforms our desires to line up with His will.

As we trust Him and feed on His faithfulness, He gives us *His* desires for our lives. He gives us *His* desires for our families. He gives us *His* desires for our nation. As our desires transform, we then pray according to His will. And He responds, "Yes, my child." But those answered prayers begin with delighting.

Likewise, Jesus says, "If you abide in me, and my words abide in you, ask whatever you wish, and it will be done for you."[4] His words have a condition. We don't just ask for whatever we want and get it. We have to start with abiding. *If* we abide in Him and *if* His words abide in us, then whatever we ask will be done. But this doesn't happen because we gain some kind of righteous favor in our abiding. It happens because our hearts transform through the abiding. Our desires change when we dwell in Him and His words remain in us.

Early in our marriage, I desperately prayed while having an ugly cry, "God, change this man. Change him! Make him love me like Jesus loves." It sounded good and right. It even sounded a little holy, because God wants our spouses to love like Jesus loves. Right? But when things stayed the same, I finally started seeking God's heart for my marriage and my home. And

---

2   Strong, "Delight" (p. 215, H6026).

3   Psalm 37:3.

4   John 15:7.

eventually my plea changed. He changed my desires: "Lord, change me. I want to experience the abundant life that Christ died to give regardless of my circumstance." That's when God mightily moved. He changed me through a breaking.

I needed breaking. Too often my eyes focused on this world. I looked to things and people that I could see and touch to fill my inner craving, especially my husband. I wanted more from life but believed that the "more" came from down here. When all the while the "more" we crave comes solely from living intimately with our Maker.

My God knew. If He had answered that initial prayer the way I thought He should, then I would have idolized my husband. I just know it. That's why God protected me. He broke me to heal me. He crushed the idol of a man's love so that I would truly know the beauty of intimacy with the Lover of my soul.

Intimate Praying

God tenderly loves us and remembers that we're needy humans. And even though He's gracious, it's important to come before Him with praise. We want to come into His holy presence with thanksgiving. Not only because He's worthy—though He is—but our souls need continual reminding of His goodness. We need to diligently remember all He's done and all He's promised. We need to remember who it is we're talking to. Otherwise we may start to sound like...my kids.

My kids need a lot of things from me. We're in that stage of life. In fact, I often feel like a maid or chauffeur or butler—me filling their requests. I talked to my daughter about it the other day. I told her that it would be nice if she could hug me before she made requests. Or maybe she could thank me for what I've already done that day, rather than hollering from the other room, "Mommy, I need such-n-such. Can you get it for me?" After she has thanked me and loved me, then she could ask for that next thing. *Or maybe she would realize she didn't really need that next thing.* "Otherwise," I told her, "I start to feel like an object." If we continually come before God with demands, we lose out on intimacy with Him. We lose out on the joy of praise.

Intimately seeking Him begins with praise and thanksgiving. But it also means we're painfully honest. It means we share everything with Him. We bear it all, running to Him before we run to anyone else. We pour out all of our fears and frustrations— continually and moment-by-moment. In essence, we allow His light to shine on the dark places within us.

Because when we voice our fears, they lose their potency. When we speak our frustrations to God, we begin the process of releasing. And when we release the difficulties, we make space in our soul to receive from Him. We *need* to receive from Him. If all I do is purge my fears and concerns at God's throne, never sitting quiet and listening to His heart, then I'm not intimate with Him. Prayer is two-way. It's a pouring out as well as a receiving.

I bet that we've all had a friend at some point in our lives who only talked about herself. Her fears and struggles dominated the conversation. But she didn't know us. Not really. She never asked about our longings. And she didn't seem interested when we tried to share. She might have called us her closest friend. She would have given us the best friends' charm necklace. *Remember those?* But we never felt intimate with her because the relationship was one-sided.

Prayer is similar. To stay intimate with Him means we receive from Him. And one way we receive in prayer is through God's Word.

Praying His Word

When we pray, we want to lay our fears and frustrations before God. But we also desperately need to hear from Him. We need to wash our concerns with the water of His Living Word. He speaks and guides through His Word. For our good and His glory, we need to meditate upon His Word.

When I hear the word "meditate," I imagine a monk in a jungle monastery, humming his way to peace. But the word "meditate" means so much more. The psalmist says, "Blessed is the man...[whose] delight is in the law of the Lord and on his law he *meditates* day and night."[5] In Hebrew, the word "meditate" means "to utter."[6] It means we aren't just *thinking* about God's Word—though we want His Word filling our minds. It means we're *speaking* God's Word. To live the blessed life, His Word needs to be on our lips.

After I've poured out all my feelings about whatever concerns me, I want to receive from Him. I need to hear from Him. So I open His Word, or His Spirit brings truths to mind, and I turn them into verbal prayers. "God, I know you work all things

---

5   Psalm 1:1-2, emphasis mine.

6   Strong, "Meditate" (p. 66, H1897).

together for the good of those who love you. And Lord, I do love you. I want to obey you. You *will* work this together for good. You will glorify Yourself through my marriage."[7]

It's true that our eyes need to read His Word. But our ears need to hear it. I'm convinced that praying His Word out loud holds power. God spoke the worlds into existence. He didn't just think the worlds into existence. When we speak, the enemy hears. We hear. And when we hear His truths, we're more prone to believe.

So we take His Word and turn it into prayers. His promises are true. As we proclaim His truths—receiving from Him—we walk in greater faith. As we remind ourselves of God's promises, we stand prepared to fight the continual spiritual battles.

There have been countless times that I've had to preach His promises out loud. I've had to receive from Him again and again in order to walk the day with the hope and peace of my God. "You promised, Lord. You *will* restore the years that the locusts have eaten. I believe You. I praise and thank You."

Intimacy with our Father grows through the giving and the receiving. Both. Not one or the other. Prayer includes receiving from Him. But it does take effort. It involves choice.

The Work of Prayer

Prayer doesn't make us righteous. Jesus makes us righteous. But prayer does make us effective. As we delight in Him, our desires transform to match His will. Therefore, the things we pray will happen. They will. And the enemy knows it. That's why he wants us to keep our mouths shut.

---

7   Romans 8:28.

While I was in the midst of writing this chapter, I had the strangest dream. Not strange as in my teeth kept falling out—though I do have that recurring dream. But strange in that it was the most spiritually heavy dream I've had in years.

In the dream, Satan was on my back. At first he took the form of a neighbor kid, but then he changed into an invisible, mean force. He bit me and caused me to writhe in pain. Until eventually the dream ended with me warring against him through a time of intense prayer.

When I woke up, I felt like I had literally fought against an enemy of darkness. In fact, I'm certain I did. But I also knew that the Lord had something for me to glean from that dream. So I sought Him for wisdom. After a time of seeking, I believed that He was reiterating the power and necessity of prayer. Power! And necessity!

The enemy knows that he cannot stand next to God's truth. He knows that when God's people call forth the will of the Father, his cohorts of darkness don't stand a chance. But he isn't nice. He doesn't give up easily. He seeks to devour anyone who reflects the glory of God. He will absolutely try to distract us from the work of prayer.

I don't always *feel* like praying. I don't always *feel* like getting up early to talk to God. Too often I'm like those sleeping disciples. Remember them? Jesus was about to be handed over for crucifixion. He was about to swallow God's cup of wrath on the cross. So He told the disciples to pray while He went further into the garden to commune with the Father in agonizing prayer. And when He came to check on them, they were asleep.

I imagine He shook His head with slight irritation—in the most perfect, holy of ways. Then He said, "So, could you not watch with me one hour? Watch and pray that you may not enter into temptation. The spirit indeed is willing, but the flesh is weak."[8]

If we are His, and His Spirit dwells within us, then we have the desire to pray. It may be buried beneath to-do lists. But His Spirit is predisposed to prayer. Yet our flesh is weak. It wrestles against the Spirit, so that the things we want to do we don't do. That's one reason to set specific prayer times.

It isn't legalism. It's wisdom. Knowing that my flesh is weak, and that I will be tired and have a long list of other excuses, I have a set time each day that I give to prayer. For me, it's first thing in the morning. I need to begin with Him. I need to start my day with His perspective. Granted, I pray continually throughout the day, but having a set time to commune with God without any distractions builds intimacy.

The act itself doesn't make me righteous. In fact, nothing I *do* makes me righteous. But as I choose to spend time in prayer—communing with my God—my faith for this day's journey grows stronger. He reminds me of His promises. And as I speak them boldly in faith, strongholds begin to crumble.[9]

Prayer is a choice we all have. Every single day I can choose to pray. I can choose to fight spiritual battles and hear from my God through prayer. I can choose to let His Word mend the broken places. It's a work I get to choose.

---

8   Matthew 26:40-41.

9   2 Corinthians 10:4.

What About Fasting?

Like prayer, the act of fasting doesn't make us more righteous. But fasting coupled with prayer is an effective, powerful discipline.

Fasting is a physical humbling. When we fast, we choose to bow ourselves low before God. We choose to afflict our souls. We choose to humble ourselves before Him and seek Him to fill us. When we set aside physical food, we see our weaknesses and become more aware of our desperation for God. When we feed our souls on the food of His Word, we gain our necessary sustenance. Because we need to feast on His truth to live.

Before God's people entered into the Promised Land, Moses recounted God's faithful working over those forty years in the wilderness. "And he humbled you and let you hunger and fed you with manna, which you did not know, nor did your fathers know, that he might make you know that *man does not live by bread alone, but man lives by every word that comes from the mouth of the LORD.*"[10]

One way or another, God's people will learn that we live by the words that come from His mouth. Whether we humble ourselves or He humbles us, we need His Word to live. Fasting helps us discover our absolute dependence.

Whenever I fast, I find that I repeat the same phrase in my spirit, especially when the bag of chips in the pantry looks especially tempting. "Lord I desire You more than I desire any physical food. I crave Your will more than any physical craving." It isn't a magical statement, but it reminds me that I'm weak without Him. It's a physical display of the inner reality: I hunger

---

10   Deuteronomy 8:3, emphasis mine.

for my God.[11] And prayers that flow from a yearning for God's will change things.

Believe What We Pray

God wants us to believe that He will give us what we ask for—specifically, the things that line up with His will:

> If any of you lacks wisdom, let him ask God, who gives generously to all without reproach, and it will be given him. But let him ask in faith, with no doubting, for the one who doubts is like a wave of the sea that is driven and tossed by the wind. For that person must not suppose that he will receive anything from the Lord; he is a double-minded man, unstable in all his ways.[12]

He calls us to faith. When we pray according to His will, we can believe that it will come to pass. We need to actively believe Him through the waiting.

I'm learning to speak more believing-prayers rather than beseeching-prayers in that season of waiting. Yes, I ask God for things and for change and for victory. But if I've already asked for something, I try to speak words of faith instead of asking for the same thing again and again. "Lord, I've already asked you to heal my marriage. To use it for Your honor. I trust that You are faithfully working that out. I trust that even in this day You are answering that prayer. Show me how I can honor You today according to its outworking."

---

11   A great resource regarding fasting is a book called *Hunger for God*, by John Piper. (Crossway Books: Illinois, 1997).

12   James 1:5-8.

Our God answers prayers. He shows Himself real and mighty through the answered prayers of His people. But prayers that most glorify Him and bring us the greatest good are prayers that line up with His will.

Whether our marriage is crumbling, our child is straying, our body is failing, our boss is criticizing, whatever it is, we're called to pray continually. He instructs us to delight in the Lord with all our heart in order that our desires would transform to line up with His good will. He hears the prayers of His children. Let's dare to believe that the prayers we make in faith will move mountains.

SMALL GROUP DISCUSSION

- Read Psalm 37:3-7. How do we delight in God?

- How have your desires changed as you have delighted in God?

- Share a time when you experienced powerful prayer. What made it powerful?

- What obstacles to prayer do you see in your own life?

- Practically speaking, how can you overcome those obstacles?

DIGGING DEEPER

God sees the heart. He isn't looking for someone who can necessarily pray with eloquence in front of a large congregation. He's looking for those who truly want to grow intimately with Him through prayer. Read Matthew 6:5-6.

Why does Jesus call them hypocrites? What did they want?

How would you describe the "secret place"?

Why does the Father reward the one who goes into the secret place with Him?

Read Matthew 6:7. How would you describe "vain repetitions"?

Read Matthew 6:8-13. "The Father knows the things you have need of before you ask." How can that truth change your prayer life?

It's because of the truth of God's intimate knowledge of us as His children that we can pray the way Jesus describes. Let's outline the aspects of Christ's prayer. How would you categorize each section?

vv. 9-10:

v. 11:

v. 12:

v. 13:

How do your own prayers compare to what Jesus described? What aspects of Jesus' prayer can you add to your own prayer life?

Close with a time of prayer. I would challenge you to get on your knees before the Lord. Humble yourself before Him. And then open your mouth in prayer. He waits to answer.

10

Walking in His redeeming power

How little chance the Holy Spirit has nowadays. The churches and missionary societies have so bound Him in red tape that they practically ask Him to sit in a corner while they do the work themselves.

Charles Thomas (C. T.) Studd

, British Protestant Christian's missionary to China, (1860-1931)

You want to know a secret? I can't do it. None of it. I can't forgive. I can't take my thoughts captive. I can't love God or my husband. I can't stay committed. I can't pray. I can't even believe Him unless His Spirit does a work within me. And that's not an exaggeration. Apart from Him birthing love and faith in and through me, I'm a hopeless mess.

I hold grudges. I overreact. I covet. I lust. I impatiently grumble. I misunderstand. I think things that would make me blush if you knew. Apart from Him, I'm a wreck. That's why I can't emphasize the gift of Himself enough. *Yes, it's time for some Spirit-talk.*

The Gift of Him Within Us
When we say "yes" to Jesus' sacrifice, the Spirit of God Himself comes to reside in us.[1] Does that make you shout a little? Think

---

1   Just to make it really clear, the gift of the Holy Spirit is only available to those who have accepted Christ as Lord of their lives. If you have never done that, then I encourage you to find a fellow Christian who can lead you into that relationship. True life begins when we say "yes" to Him.

about it. The almighty God Himself—the One who raised Jesus from the dead—comes to live *in* us. We become His home—His temple. He comes to guide, teach, and bless. He comes to make us alive from the inside out. He comes to *empower* us to walk out this high calling of selfless love.

Before Jesus ascended into heaven, He told His disciples that they would receive power when the Holy Spirit comes upon them. Power. Like dynamite power. And when the Spirit fell on them at Pentecost, power fell. No longer did they clump together questioning what was to come; they became bold witnesses to the work of Christ. They faced councils and proclaimed Jesus' resurrection. They gave themselves to be martyred and sold all they had. They healed diseases and cast out demons. Power fell when His Spirit came. And power still falls when His Spirit comes to dwell within a believer.

So why don't we experience His outworking? Why do pockets of the church appear faithless and weak? Why are believing families falling apart at the seams? Honestly, I don't think we understand what it means to live filled by His Spirit.

It says in Ephesians that after we hear the word of Christ and believe, His Spirit seals us.[2] That word "seals" means "to stamp with a signet or private mark for security or preservation."[3] God places His mark upon us. He seals us with Himself in order to transform us into holy vessels of His love.

But it doesn't stop with His sealing. Even though we're sealed, we still have to work out our salvation.[4] We still have our

---

2   Ephesians 1:13.

3   Strong, "Seal" (p. 244, G4972).

4   Philippians 2:12-13.

flesh. And our flesh wrestles against the Spirit. Our flesh self-
ishly says, "Mine." It wants its own way and demands its rights.
It fights against crucifixion. That's why we have to seek Him for
His continual *filling*.

Filled with His Spirit

He *seals* us with His Spirit one time. When we accept the sacrifice of Christ, by faith, He seals us. It's a done deal. But we're
filled continually. We have to keep on being filled. In fact, every
hour of every day we choose to walk according to His Spirit or
walk according to our flesh. We have that choice. And believe
me, it shows.

If I'm submitting to His Spirit's filling, then His fruit shows.
I love selflessly. I have joy even in what should be despair.
I experience peace through the middle of a crashing storm (and
whiny children). I'm slow to anger and patient with the process.
I do good things for my husband even if he doesn't deserve it that
day. I'm kind with my words and expressions. I remain faithful
even if I'm betrayed. I gently handle the other's soul. And I live
self-controlled.[5] Those moments are true beauty.

But then there's my flesh. If I'm giving in to the lust of my
flesh, ugly thoughts and bitter things fill me. And yes, they come
out. I walk around with a chip on my shoulder and a smirk on
my face. I waste precious time worrying about what may happen
tomorrow...or next year. I want life to obey my plans; and I want
it yesterday. I criticize others and speak rude things because "if

---

5   Galatians 5:22-23.

I don't tell them, who will?" I run away and rough up the hearts around me. Do you get the picture? When I give into my flesh, Jesus can't be seen. It's just selfish me.

But in Christ, we don't have to stay chained to our flesh responses. He died on the cross to free us from our old, fleshly ways. We now have a choice—follow the flesh or live filled by His Spirit. The question is, "How do I live filled by Him?"

First, we need to keep perspective. We all have weaknesses. And until we breathe our last breath on this earth, we will continue to have weaknesses. That's why His grace amazes. When we fail again and again, He still says loving things over us. He still forgives. He still keeps us sealed with His Spirit. We need to remember His mercies when we fall into that same flesh pit. In fact, the flesh pit just reveals what everyone else already knows about us: We ain't God.

We also want to remember that those weak, flesh areas are the exact places where God wants to fill us full of Himself. Our weakness can become our greatest strength because His power can overwhelm our meager flesh.[6] When we have to forgive our spouse *again* and it feels like we haven't an ounce of mercy left, His power can enable us to free them from our personal judgment. Our weaknesses can become our greatest victories.

But life is still hard and our flesh still rises up. So, along with remembering true things, it's important to identify our "flesh triggers." We all have them. They're situations or relationships that

---

6   2 Corinthians 12:8-10.

trigger a flesh response from us. One of mine inevitably hits me when I drive our mini-van.

I always swore I would never drive a mini-van. But alas, three kids later, I drive a van. And when we're cruising around, these three little people of mine often feel the need to aggravate one another. They grab each other and holler things like "stop touching me." And after I give a few kind reminders to love one another, that warm-frustrated feeling rises up. And if I give into my flesh turmoil, I overreact. Because loud whininess triggers my flesh. *Can I get a witness?*

When I give in to my flesh trigger—instead of walking filled with His Spirit—I quench His Spirit. I grieve Him when I disobey. And when I grieve Him, I won't experience His power. *A travesty.*

He seals us once, but He fills us continually. He fills us in order to enable us to walk out this season of life with victory. He does it when I'm in a mini-van and He does it when my marriage crumbles. But unless I walk in His power, I will never experience victory in spite of circumstance.

A Re-Stirring

If we find ourselves numb to His filling—weak in our faith and lacking His fruit—then we can stir Him up within us. That's what Paul tells Timothy to do, "Fan into flame the gift of God, which is in you through the laying on of my hands, for God gave us a spirit not of fear but of power and love and self-control."[7] Stir Him up. To stir

---

7   2 Timothy 1:6-7.

Him up is to believe that He will fill us full. For me, that looks like a personal mini-preaching session. And it begins with confession.

If possible, I break away when I've succumbed to a flesh trigger. I pull the van into an empty parking lot and get out to talk to God. *Yep, literally.* I confess my flesh response as sin, even if I've confessed that exact same sin two hours before. Thankfully, God remembers we're dust. No sin is too much. It doesn't matter how many times we've failed. If we honestly confess our sins to Him with a humble heart, then He forgives and cleanses.[8] That's a promise. Humble confession stirs His power.

After we confess, we can then give His Spirit full reign over our soul, mind and body. We can give Him ourselves and believe Him to fill us. We may want to ask if there is anything else within us that hinders His outpouring in our lives. And then we may want to declare our absolute desperation: "I can't do it, Lord. It has to be You in me."

Once I've declared my desperation, I start preaching true things about my God. I remind myself—out loud—that the Spirit of the Most High indwells me. The power of my God enables me to walk this moment with wisdom and joy. Then I praise Him. And I thank Him. Because praise and thanksgiving stir Him up. Finally, I declare my belief that He will faithfully fill me. And by His grace, He stirs. It doesn't always happen immediately, but as I keep believing Him to fill, He fills. And I change.

Only then do I truly forgive. Only then am I able to take my thoughts captive to truth. Only then can I release control. Only then do I live free.

---

8   1 John 1:9.

One Place To Begin

If talking about God's indwelling Spirit is new to you, that's OK. In fact, it's exciting, because today might be the start of a powerful journey.

I've mentioned that after my rebellious college years, God graciously wooed me back to Himself. *In spite of me.* He set me on fire for Him. But after a while in His Word, I realized that I didn't "know" His Spirit very well. I felt like I "knew" the Father and I "knew" Jesus—as much as you can know two infinite persons of the Trinity—but His Spirit seemed distant and detached. So, as childish as it sounds, I simply prayed, "Father, I want to know Your Spirit within me. I want to experience the power of Your Holy Spirit." And over time, He began to show Himself active in my life. He showed me what it meant to trust Him and be filled by Him. And in some ways, it was preparation for the valleys to come.

Our marriage journey has been rough. *We'd both testify to that.* But it hasn't been purposeless. God not only used it, but I fully believe He *meant* it for my transformation and for the transformation of our home. Through the trial, He proved His sufficiency. He further convinced me of the truth of His Word. And by His absolute grace, I imperfectly dared to believe Him.

He Has To Do It

I feel a mix of emotion as I type the last few paragraphs of this book. Part of me feels heavy because even after trekking through all these words, I can't fix that difficult situation. I can't fix your marriage. I can't bring that prodigal home. I can't heal your broken body or crushed heart. I can't change your desires. I can't make you believe.

All I can do is testify. I can tell you how I have sought after God through one of the darkest seasons of my life. I can give you tips for your thought life. I can lay out His commands to forgive. And I can share how brilliantly He shows up each and every day through each and every storm. But ultimately, the victory comes as an outworking of His Spirit. *He* opens our eyes. *He* changes our minds. *He* guides our feet and convicts our hearts. *He* does the work.

So, I simply pray. And trust. I pray that He moves mightily in you and through you. Did you catch that? *Mightily!* I pray you believe Him to do wildly redemptive things. I pray He shows off through your home and your kids. I pray you leave deep imprints of Him.

Wherever He has you, my friend—whether it's the deepest, darkest valley of your life, or the highest mountaintop adventure—He *has* you. If you've named Him "Lord" then you are His and nothing can separate you from His love. Nothing. Dare to believe. Victory and abundance are yours for the taking regardless of your circumstance. Because He promised. And He always comes through.

SMALL GROUP DISCUSSION

• What are your flesh triggers?

• Practically speaking, what can you do the next time one of those triggers comes?

• Share a time when you experienced His filling.

• What is one area of your life (one situation or relationship) where you hope God will do a mighty work?

DIGGING DEEPER

We can't do any of it apart from Him. And I know that you want to love like Jesus loves and serve like He serves. I know you do because you read this book. And you have a yearning in you from Him, like a piece of clay desperate for its Potter.

So here's the amazing news: we can't do it, but He can. And He does! By His Spirit, He loves through us. He enables us to forgive. He prompts us to serve selflessly, with a happy heart. Let's read some passages that tell us more about this gift of the Holy Spirit.

Spend some time with the following passages and note what you learn about the Holy Spirit (You may want to take a few days to glean from the texts.):

Luke 4:1-2

John 14:15-17

John 16:13-15

Acts 1:1-8

Acts 2:1-4

Acts 2:38-39

Acts 4:8-13, 18-20

1 Corinthians 12:4-11

Ephesians 4:25-32

List one or two key areas of your life in which you need to depend on His indwelling Spirit:

What are some verses that you can use as "weapons in the warfare" when your flesh battles against His Spirit, specifically regarding the areas you listed above?

After reading this book, what are three "takeaways" that you want His Spirit to seal upon your heart?

The Envy of Eve

Finding Contentment in
a Covetous World

MELISSA B. KRUGER

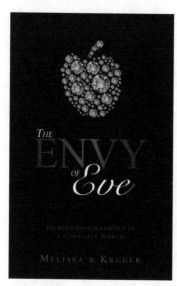

ISBN 978-1-84550-775-6

What's truly at the heart of our desires?
The Envy of Eve guides readers to understand how desires grow into covetousness and what happens when this sin takes power in our hearts. Covetousness chokes out the fruit of the Spirit in our lives, allowing discontentment to bloom. The key to overcoming is to get to the root of our problem: unbelief – a mistrust of God's sovereignty and goodness. An ideal resource for deeper study or group discussion.

In an age and culture where we all tend to have an overdeveloped sense of entitlement, this book makes a brilliant diagnosis that goes right to the heart of the problem.

Ann Benton
Author and family conference speaker, Guildford, England

With I've-been-there understanding and been-in-the-Word insight, Melissa B. Kruger helps us to look beneath the surface of our discontent, exposing our covetous hearts to the healing light of God's Word.

Nancy Guthrie
Author of Seeing Jesus in the Old Testament Bible Study Series

Melissa leads and creates Bible study material and is greatly involved in the women's ministry at her church in Charlotte, North Carolina. Her husband, Michael, is the president of The Reformed Theological Seminary in Charlotte.

I Am My Sister's Keeper

Reaching out to Wounded Women

DENISE GEORGE

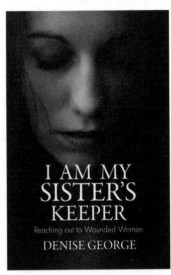

ISBN 978-1-84550-717-6

I Am My Sister's Keeper tenderly addresses issues like broken relationships and divorce; unforgiveness; loneliness; spouse abuse; and loss and grief. Through biblical stories and contemporary stories of wounded women, George's advice guides readers in how to pray, offer a listening ear, share from their own experiences and encourage others with God's promises. A complete Bible study guide makes this an ideal resource for groups of women to study together.

With the love of Jesus poured out through his followers, hurting women begin to overcome painful circumstances. Through our hearts and our hands, God still heals wounded women.

I found I Am My Sister's Keeper *a genuinely Christian response to particular issues that cause much suffering among many women in today's world. It motivated me to care more deeply for women I meet by sensitively listening to their stories, praying for and with them, showing practical love, and especially by sharing God's love for them in Jesus.*

Moya Woodhouse
Faculty wife at Moore College, Sydney, Australia

Denise George is an internationally popular writer and speaker best known for creative Biblical application. Denise is married to Dr. Timothy George, executive editor of Christianity Today and founding Dean of Beeson Divinity School in Birmingham, Alabama.

Christian Focus Publications

Our mission statement –

STAYING FAITHFUL

In dependence upon God we seek to impact the world through literature faithful to His infallible Word, the Bible. Our aim is to ensure that the Lord Jesus Christ is presented as the only hope to obtain forgiveness of sin, live a useful life and look forward to heaven with Him.

Our Books are published in four imprints:

CHRISTIAN
FOCUS

popular works including biographies, commentaries, basic doctrine and Christian living.

CHRISTIAN
HERITAGE

books representing some of the best material from the rich heritage of the church.

MENTOR

books written at a level suitable for Bible College and seminary students, pastors, and other serious readers. The imprint includes commentaries, doctrinal studies, examination of current issues and church history.

CF4•K

children's books for quality Bible teaching and for all age groups: Sunday school curriculum, puzzle and activity books; personal and family devotional titles, biographies and inspirational stories – Because you are never too young to know Jesus!

Christian Focus Publications Ltd,
Geanies House, Fearn, Ross-shire,
IV20 1TW, Scotland, United Kingdom.
www.christianfocus.com